Go and Do Likewise

Catholic Social Teaching
in Action

GO do and LIKEWISE

CATHOLIC SOCIAL TEACHING IN ACTION

Mia Crosthwaite

TWENTY THIRD 23rd
PUBLICATIONS

Twenty-Third Publications
A Division of Bayard
One Montauk Avenue, Suite 200
New London, CT 06320
(860) 437-3012 or (800) 321-0411
www.23rdpublications.com

ISBN-10: 1-58595-548-5
ISBN 978-1-58595-548-0

Library of Congress Catalog Card Number: 2005934263
Printed in the U.S.A.

To Henry,
who shows me how it's done

Acknowledgments

This book felt like a wellspring coming out of me, and just like all the workings of God in the world, it was a community effort. There were many who were part of the process. I am especially grateful to Eileen Lawrence, the first one to see my writing and a source of great insight. She is a writer's best friend with her regular question, "What do you have for me to read?" She asks the tough questions and is always generous with honesty. My writing is so much wiser because of her.

Writing is a vocation that took a long time for me to own. A significant event for me was attending the Catholic Writers Retreat at Redemptorist Renewal Center, lead by Fr. Tom Santa and made possible by the Catholic Book Publishers Association. I am deeply grateful to them. Another significant event was attending a Called and Gifted Retreat, developed by the Catherine of Siena Institute and lead by Debbie Oaas, Carol McGee, and Bill Kearley. I remember my surprise when Debbie said, doubtfully, "You didn't score high in writing," and Carol said, "You might want to do some discerning on writing."

This book would not have been possible without my own formation in Catholic social teaching. When I became Catholic, it was the social teachings of the church that let me know I was home. I am thankful to the Boise Catholic Worker community, Boisesans for Peace and Justice, Jim Holden, Gard Hanks, Kathy Krewer, Rap and Leona Howell, Marie Hoff, and Fr. Hugh Feiss for their teaching in both word and action.

I am deeply grateful to those who reviewed the manuscript and gave me precious insights that helped make it better: Br. Selby

Coffman, Carol McGee, Jim Holden, Kathy and Henry Krewer, Sr. Helene Higgins, Bette Wunderle, Melanie Swenson, Sr. Arlene Ellis, and Cathy Cobb.

In everything that I do, my husband, Brian, is in the background making it all possible. The joy in my heart is in large part due to spending my life with him and our amazing children. Their love, support, and acceptance shape the person that I am and fuel the energy of my life. I am so blessed to be able to spend my life loving them.

I dedicate this book to Henry Krewer, whose constant example and challenge bring out the best in me. I hear the word of God most clearly in his voice.

Contents

What Is Social Justice?

Talking with people about social justice is like talking about salvation—everybody means something different when they say these words. Some people mean charity: "I love social justice, so I give groceries to the food bank." Others mean social action: "We're going to organize a letter-writing campaign in the name of social justice." Some use the term to refer to the whole body of Catholic social teaching. Sometimes people use the term to mean something closer to warfare: "We marched for social justice against XYZ Company." And some people just run away: "I don't believe in that social justice stuff."

In order to talk about doing social justice, we first need to find some common understanding on exactly what it is. The *Catechism of the Catholic Church* says that "society ensures social justice when it provides the conditions that allow associations or individuals to obtain what is their due, according to their nature and their vocation. Social justice is linked to the common good and the exercise of authority" (§1928).

Social justice starts with God and God's example for us. The Old Testament reveals a God full of justice and mercy. God intervened in history and politics to free the Hebrews from slavery in Egypt, having mercy on their plight and demanding justice for their condition. After leading them to the promised land, God instructed the nation of Israel to divide the land justly, based on the number of families, so that each family had what they needed.

Biblical justice is essentially divine fairness—we get what we deserve—whereas biblical mercy is essentially divine compassion—we get what we *don't* deserve. Paradoxically, God is both. The prophet Sirach declared: "He who lives forever created the whole universe; the Lord alone is just…the Lord is patient with them and pours out his mercy upon them" (Sirach 18:1, 11). The psalmist proclaimed: "The Lord works vindication and justice for all who are oppressed….The Lord is merciful and gracious, slow to anger and abounding in steadfast love" (Psalms 103:6, 8).

Biblical justice flows from divine love, from God's vision for the world and God's judgment of fairness. When I read the first chapters of Genesis, it can feel like God is speaking directly to me; but more so, God is speaking to us as a human community. God created the whole world for the human family to share, each having enough. God did not gift the world to individual people but instead to all of humanity with the expectation that it be shared, like parents leaving their estate to all five children and expecting them to divide it fairly and compassionately.

Biblical justice means that our sharing includes every human person because God's sharing includes every human person. The land and resources created by God are not ours; they are God's. A deed to a piece of property doesn't make it ours; deeds are issued by human beings. In the Old Testament we learn that all the land belonged to God and was only held in trust by the people. That's why Yahweh decreed that every fifty years the land be returned to the original families. "It shall be a jubilee for you: you shall return, every one of you, to your property every one of you to your family" (Leviticus 25:10).

Almost from the beginning of their existence, human beings have failed to live up to God's justice. We know this because the prophets often ranted about it. (Prophets, like parents, only correct when there is a problem. You never say, "don't eat the dirt," until the child actually puts the dirt in his or her mouth.) Isaiah said: "Learn to do good; seek justice, rescue the oppressed, defend the orphan, plead for the widow" (Isaiah 1:17). Jeremiah said: "Do no wrong or violence to the alien, the orphan, and the widow" (Jeremiah 22:3). Micah said: "What does the Lord require of you but to do justice, and to love kindness, and to walk humbly with your God?" (Micah 6:8).

Jesus echoed the call of the prophets. Everything about the kingdom of heaven is firmly grounded in divine justice and mercy, but it can be confusing to our twenty-first century ears. The parable of the workers in the vineyard feels unfair to our sensibilities (Matthew 20:1–16) because the people who show up at the end of the day are paid the same as those who have been working all day long. It's not fair! What about the prodigal son who got the fatted calf while his well-behaved brother was scolded (Luke 15:11–32)? There is something in the stories that remains shrouded in a fog for us.

Social justice is the systematic face of human rights: the right to life, food, health, decent housing, education, work, freedom, and so on. We don't earn these rights. They are ours by birth and arise out of our creation—every one of us is created in the image and likeness of God. Whether we labor all day long or just a few minutes at the end, we all have the right to food and shelter. Whether we are born in wealth or in dire poverty, we all have the right to education. Whether we are an innocent little baby, a productive worker, or a guilty criminal, we all have the right to life. Justice is recognizing and respecting the rights of all people.

Thomas Jefferson understood rights, and he called them inalienable. Just as rights can't be earned, they can't be discarded either. If we believe that a criminal act can negate a person's right to life, then it was never a right to begin with; it was a privilege. What makes something a right is that it is inviolable. A person cannot give up their rights; they can only be complicit in allowing them to be violated. Because rights originate from God, injustice is an affront to the Creator.

What we call social justice in the Scriptures is often God fixing the problems people created. Throughout the Bible God calls for special care for the orphan, the widow, and the alien—the victims of social injustice both then and now. Today we say children, women, and immigrants, but it's the same people who are suffering. God's special care for people isn't the result of loving them better; it is because they are being hurt by God's other children. When a little girl is hurt by her brother, their parents run to comfort the girl and pay special attention to her. Similarly, the orphans, the widows, and the aliens receive special attention from God simply because they are hurting.

The problem of social justice is a complicated one. If solving it were as simple as stopping one person from stealing another person's food, it would be easy to work for social justice. But the world is much more complicated than that. Quite often rights are not denied directly; they are taken away subtly and, therefore, much more pervasively. We have built social structures such as governments, economies, families, and communities, as well as ways of thinking, such as sexism and racism, that deny people their rights. We have created a world that leaves people out.

For example, in my hometown a homeless man received a $125 ticket for sleeping in the park. Because he couldn't afford to pay the fine, he didn't go to his court date. He was cited with failure to appear in court, a warrant was issued for his arrest, and he was sent to jail. In an indirect but very real way, our criminal justice system incarcerated this man for being homeless.

Another example involves the health care system in the United States, which is based on access to employer-based health insurance or an individual's ability to pay their own costs. A self-employed woman in my state lived without health insurance because it was too expensive and too difficult to get as an individual. When she was in her mid-forties, she was diagnosed with breast cancer. Because she had been unable to buy health insurance, she was faced with the choice of exhausting her family's life savings to pay for treatment, or using that money to send her children to college. She chose not to pursue treatment. In an indirect but very real way, our health care system was an accomplice to her early death.

Social Justice and Christianity

If you mention social justice at church, before long you will hear: "I don't have time to do one more thing." These Christian people love God, but because social justice hasn't been part of their faith life in the past, they assume it is something extra.

For a Christian to say they don't have time for social justice is like saying they don't have time to attend church, read the Bible, or pray. It's like saying they don't have time to love. Social justice is part of the very essence of being Christian. It is walking the walk and talking the talk. According to the United States Conference of Catholic Bishops, "the church teaches that social justice is an integral part of evangelization, a constitutive dimension of preaching the gospel, and an essential part of the church's mission" (*Communities of Salt and Light*, 1993).

Social justice is really about living a life that reflects the model of Jesus. It is about those actions that reveal who we really are. Being a follower of Jesus means taking his teachings seriously. It is not enough to call Jesus "Savior" if our treatment of others is unjust. "Not everyone who says to me, 'Lord, Lord,' will enter the kingdom of heaven, but only the one who does the will of my Father in heaven" (Matthew 7:21). If we talk the talk without walking the walk, we do injury to the gospel.

Jesus was asked what we are to do to inherit eternal life. He answered: "You shall love the Lord your God with all your heart, and with all your soul, with all your strength, and with all your mind; and your neighbor as yourself" (Luke 10:27). The instruction to love God and neighbor is spoken in one sentence, almost as one phrase. Our love of God is manifest in our love of neighbor, and vice versa.

Many Christians misunderstand this commandment as a directive that love of God *should* be exhibited as love of neighbor. I believe this Scripture is not a directive but rather, a statement of fact. When a person truly loves God, they cannot help but love their neighbor. It is like saying that when the sun rises, the day warms. "Those who say, 'I love God' and hate their brothers or sisters are liars; for those who do not love a brother or sister whom they have seen, cannot love God whom they have not seen" (1 John 4:20). When we love God, we love God's creation, and we love that most precious part of God's creation: human beings.

Jesus was harsh with people who followed religious laws but didn't practice justice and mercy. "Woe to you, scribes and Pharisees, hypocrites! For you tithe mint, dill, and cumin, and have neglected the weightier matters of the law: justice and mercy and faith" (Matthew 23:23). His warning to them is a warning to us when we insist on orthodoxy but neglect justice and compassion in our daily living.

Recognizing that this love of neighbor is integral, the very foundation of Christianity, raises the question: who is my neighbor? Who are these people I should love? Jesus answered these questions in the parable of the Good Samaritan, when he defined "neighbor" as "'the one who showed him mercy.' Jesus said to him, 'Go and do likewise.'" (Luke 10:37). Our call to live as neighbor to everyone, to treat all with mercy and compassion, is part of the call of discipleship.

Never has there been more of a need to embrace this teaching than now. At the Second Vatican Council, the church fathers wrote: "Today, there is an inescapable duty to make ourselves the neighbor of every individual, without exception, and to take positive steps to help a neighbor whom we encounter" (§27, *Guadium et Spes: Pastoral Constitution on the Church in the Modern World*).

We must be cautious in asking, "Who is my neighbor?" We tend to want to classify people as "us" or "them." We want to include some people as "us," the ones we will treat as neighbor with compassion and love, and exclude others as "them," the ones we can ignore and blindly degrade. This is exactly the type of thinking Jesus condemned. "Truly I tell you, just as you did it to one of the least of these who are members of my family, you did it to me" (Matthew 25:40). Just as our love of God is consistent and persistent, so too is our work for social justice.

Many people, especially those who aren't poor, interpret Jesus' tidings of good news for the poor as exclusively a promise for wealth in the afterlife after enduring an earthly life of poverty. But Jesus' good news for the poor was much more immediate: the good news was that they would be poor no longer. Jesus said: "Blessed are you who are poor, for yours is the kingdom of God; Blessed are you who are hungry now, for you will be filled" (Luke 6:20–21). When the poor inherit the land, they are no longer poor! When the hungry are filled, they are no longer hungry!

Mary's magnificat echoes this theme: "He has filled the hungry with good things, and sent the rich away empty" (Luke 1:53). In *Doing Faithjustice*, Fred Kammer, S.J., former head of Catholic Charities USA, wrote: "By responding or not to the least of Jesus' sisters and brothers, those under judgment have responded—or not—to Christ. Without the doing of justice, Christ remains unknown!"

Being a follower of Jesus means accepting his mission as our own. If Jesus came to bring good news to the poor, then we, too, must bring good news to the poor. We, the body of Christ, continue to minister to the same earthly needs of people that Jesus ministered to: hunger (feeding of the multitudes), healing (performing miracles), and justice (befriending tax collectors and prostitutes). As Avery Dulles wrote in his groundbreaking work, *Models of the Church*: "The church's mission, in the perspective of [servant] theology, is not primarily to gain new recruits for its own ranks, but rather to be of help to all men, wherever they are."

Jesus told us to watch his actions. In the gospel of John, the crowds ask him to tell them if he was the Christ. Instead, he instructs them to watch him. "The works that I do in my Father's name testify to me" (John 10:25). The same is true for us. The works we do testify to the one we follow. Our actions reveal what we really believe; they tell the truth of who we really are. Just because we say something, doesn't make it true. Sometimes our actions can be self-revealing. We tell ourselves that we're not sexist but we don't attend lectures by well-spoken and educated women. We tell ourselves that we're not racist while we support laws that treat Mexican immigrants harshly.

It wasn't just hurting people that Jesus warned against; he also warned against benefiting from injustice. If any person is rich while poverty still exists, then that rich person is part of the problem. Jesus told the rich young man to sell everything he had, give the money to the poor, and come follow him (Luke 18:18–23). The parable of Lazarus and the rich man is even clearer. The rich man, enjoying his wealth while Lazarus suffered poverty outside his door, ended up in torment while Lazarus ended up in bliss (Luke 16:19–31). The rich man's sin was that he did nothing while benefiting from an unjust economic system.

We are often convinced that the current system is the only way, especially when we benefit from the current system. We have developed elaborate defense mechanisms and often state, correctly, that we didn't personally create the oppression. But we run into trouble when we absolve ourselves from all responsibility. We begin conversion when we recognize that when we benefit from oppression, we are part of the problem.

The first step in working for social justice is to see it. These benefits that we enjoy make it that much more difficult to see social injustice: we are motivated to remain blind. Being Christian means looking for where we benefit from social injustice and confronting our own defense mechanisms. When we pray to Jesus for "ears to hear" (Mark 4:9, Luke 8:8), it may feel like we are praying for our own condemnation. The gospels call us to see the world through God's eyes, to find a new understanding of fairness and justice that matches God's, to exercise mercy freely and compassion constantly.

In fact, turning away from this responsibility can rightly be called sinful. Catherine Harmer wrote in *The Compassionate Community*: "It is one thing to fail to live up to what one believes, as an individual and a society. It is much worse to know what is demanded and to subvert that call by preaching a message of uncompassionate, uncaring oppression of the poor." As Christians, we must be attentive to those sins of omission where we are called to help the poor and we answer no. If we turn away, Jesus' story of Lazarus and the rich man should rightly strike fear in our hearts. The rich man did nothing to hurt Lazarus; he just didn't help, and he ended up in torment. God doesn't buy our self-deception when we say it is not our fault.

We can change social systems. We, as a people, created these systems, and we can change them. Jesus told us that we have the power to change things. We have enormous influence over these systems that are no more than human constructions. We can support these structures, or we can erode them like rivers carving out canyons. We can go on benefiting from social injustices, or we can chip away at those systems until they fall into holy order.

Doing It

Your heart is on fire, and you know you want to follow this way of Jesus, but you're having difficulty getting started. What do you do? We are people of action, and we like to do things. We want to do the things Jesus commanded us to do; we want our actions to reflect what we truly believe.

There are thousands of little things you can do to start living social justice right now. Some take no time, and some take a little bit of time. All involve a reorientation toward God, a conversion to the way that Jesus taught, a dedication to walking the path that God has laid before us. All presuppose that our thinking begin with the common good rather than personal gain.

We are a very individualistic people, and that individualism has led to great things: our dedication to human rights, initiative, and personal freedom. But we can also use individualism as a weapon, blaming people for their poverty rather than seeing them as victims of a system, or exclusively blaming post-abortive women for the death of their babies rather than seeing both the babies and the women as victims of a system. For social justice to be real, it must always focus on a world where it's easy to be righteous, where everyone enjoys and easily exercises their rights.

When Jesus saw some wealthy people contributing to the temple out of their surplus, he spurned them, while holding up a poor widow who only gave two small coins. "Truly I tell you, this poor widow has put in more than all of them; for all of them have contributed out of their abundance, but she out of her poverty has put in all she had to live on" (Luke 21:1–4). If we are only willing to pursue social justice out of our surplus, then it is shallow. When social justice is a pervasive and persistent part of our living, then it is real and genuine.

We must be careful, however, that our work for the poor and the oppressed comes from the perspective that "they" are part of "us," that we are helping our own brothers and sisters. We must be careful not to judge the poor, especially because so many of us misunderstand their plight. Too often, we suffer the prejudices handed down by our English forebears, who established debtors prisons to incarcerate the poor for being poor. We continue to equate poverty with being lazy, undependable, and dangerous. We hold onto the idea of the "deserving" poor as the only ones worthy of help. Yet the poor that Jesus held up as blessed were the ones in dire, long-lasting, and institutionalized poverty.

Doing social justice involves both taking action and changing thinking, and so there are two different types of suggestions in this book. One involves an activity or concrete effect, and the other is about personal conversion.

Many people feel that just learning about social justice and changing their attitudes is a waste of time. But ideas are powerful. When our attitudes change, they affect those around us, even though we may never see the results. Ideas are infectious and forceful. Remember, the chief priests and scribes wanted Jesus' death because of his ideas.

Changing attitudes flow into actions that include both private action and public action. Fundamentally, there is no significant difference between the two; both are important. Private actions, by definition, are actions that we undertake personally. Public actions are not separate from ourselves, but they are the collective work of groups of people. A public structure can feel so much bigger than one person that we forget that the structure is nothing more than the creation of people. Politics is merely the expression of a group's ideas in a governmental setting. It is not separate from us; it is part of our public identity. The idea that Christians should not be involved in politics is to reject part of ourselves and therefore, to reject part of our Christian mission.

God's justice does indeed originate with God, but it requires our cooperation and our participation. God didn't deliver the Israelites from slavery singlehandedly; Moses helped. God asks each one of us to cooperate with the glorious vision for the world. Our task is to accept, and have faith that we are capable of doing what God asks us to do. "Who gives speech to mortals? Who makes them mute or deaf, seeing or blind? Is it not I, the Lord? Now go, and I will be with your mouth and teach you what you are to speak" (Exodus 4:11–12).

Be aware that confronting social injustice means coming up against those who benefit directly and indirectly from the current system. History is crowded with examples of enormous violence that resulted from injustice being confronted, for example, the French Revolution, the American Civil War, the Russian Revolution, and the murder of thousands in Central America over the past fifty years. Sooner or later, helping oppressed people will meet with resistance and bring struggles and pain.

In moments of suffering and self-doubt, we can look to Jesus. In the paschal mystery, he gave us a model of how to deal with torment. Jesus suffered, died, and was raised from the dead. As Christians, we remember that in our pain and suffering, God is there with us. Suffering is never the end of the story. In the end God will save us and redeem us. We may be vilified for our advocacy. We may discover that our best intentions turned out to be ineffective. We may realize that we were wrong. We will be tempted to give up. Yet with the grace of God, we will continue, having experienced the joy of the resurrection and the satisfaction that comes from living a life in partnership with the divine.

Getting Started

The bishops, in their wisdom, have laid the foundation for Catholic social teaching, but living out these social teachings is the vocation of every baptized person. In this book are ideas that flesh out these teachings with activities and suggestions that can be done in five, ten, or twenty minutes. Our lives are busy, but most of us are capable of spending five minutes doing something we haven't done before. Some days you may only have five minutes, but some days you'll have more. The ideas are listed by time so you can easily go to the section that will work for you.

The ideas in this book are a way to start consciously living out social justice. Most people find they are are already doing things that live out the church's social teachings, and knowing that makes them confident to do more. They also find that in exploring ideas and doing activities, they come up with new ways of their own for living out the church's social teaching.

Some of the ideas in this book will strike a chord with you, and you will be excited to pursue them. If you find yourself disgreeing with an idea, just pass it by. The goal here is not to try every idea listed, but to find the ones that are meaningful for you.

Where public policies are addressed at the federal level, I have indicated that you contact your congressmen. Where they are addressed at the state level, I have indicated you contact your legislators, and so forth. Please keep in mind that some of the specifics may be different in your area. If you're not sure, contact the people mentioned, and they will point you in the right direction. (Make sure to always include your name, address, and phone number when writing to an elected official.)

This book can be used individually, in a family, in small groups, or in a parish.

• For individual use

Read a bit each week, searching for one thing you can do that week. The next week, find a different idea. This is an especially good spiritual exercise during Lent—not with the intent of doing something special for Lent, but for building a new way of being that begins in Lent and transforms your life.

• For family use

For those who are raising a family, doing things together is the most meaningful way to learn, but it can also be challenging. We have to choose activities that make sense to children of different ages, while not watering the message down so much that it loses all meaning. The good news is that children are intuitive and learn quickly just by watching what is important to you.

If your children are young, pick one suggestion in each chapter that seems feasible, and do it together. Make sure your children are physically involved in the doing, not just watching.

If you have older children, present three suggestions each month, and decide together which one you will do. Afterward, spend some time talking together. How did you feel? Who was helped? What did God think of it? What did you learn?

• For use in a small group

Underneath Catholic social teaching is the paradigm-shifting message of the gospel. In a small group, the work is reinforced by the efforts of each member. Here are some ways to proceed.

1. Assign a chapter that can be read before you next gather together as a group.

2. At the next gathering, invite each person to share the ideas that excited them. Continue discussion to draw out the reasons behind that excitement. If the group will be acting on ideas together, discuss several possibilities until you agree on one or two ideas. Your discussion may surface other ideas that also live out the specific teaching.

3. Create an action plan of what will be done by the next gathering. Assign people to specific tasks.

4. When you next gather together, reflect on the implementation of the activity. How did it change the spiritual life of the group? What aspect of social justice teaching did the activity embody? Did this activity meet people's expectations? Is follow-up needed? If so, what will be done?

• For use with a parish social justice committee or pastoral council

Using this book in a parish social justice committee or pastoral council can help the parish enflesh the church's social teachings. Here are some steps you could use at a meeting.

1. Assign a chapter that can be read before the next meeting.

2. At that meeting, invite each person to share the ideas that excited them, and why.

3. Continue discussion until consensus arises around one or two ideas. Your discussion may surface other ideas that also live out the specific teaching.

4. Create an action plan of what will be done by the next meeting. Assign people to specific tasks.

5. At the following meeting, reflect on how the implementation went. How has it changed the spiritual life of the parish? In its implementation, did the act embody the social justice teaching? Does the implementation need to be modified? Continue this action-reflection process for one or more meetings.

• For use in a parish

In the whole parish setting, this book can be used to reach many people. While discussions can't occur in the same way, conversation can be encouraged as the whole parish moves through the book. Here is one idea on how to use it in a parish.

1. Three months prior to beginning, announce that the whole parish will be focusing on Catholic social teaching. Talk about it in pulpit announcements and bulletin articles. Plan some homilies on action as an honest expression of belief and faith as expressed through works.

2. Do one theme per month. All month long, print the theme in the bulletin along with three ideas or actions that people could carry out. You might want to use some suggestions for individuals, and others that can be done in groups.

3. Work the theme into liturgical preaching throughout the month. You may also want to put up posters that have the social justice teaching written out on them in the narthex or other common area.

5. Ask people to continue to reflect on each social justice teaching and how they can live it out in their own lives, both personally and in groups.

Prayer

Use this prayer alone or in a group.

Lord,

> God of the Israelites delivered from exile,
> God of Jesus who came to save the world,
> God of oppressed people everywhere,
>> today we pray for the courage to live the lives you gave us.

We pray for the passion and energy of your Holy Spirit,
> we pray for the peace that comes from
>> living our lives following you,
> and we pray for the joy of seeing you face to face.

We ask that when we fail,
> you will comfort and guide us.

We pray that in our success, we are always humble.

We ask that you heal us of all indifference and apathy.

Lord, we are here to serve you and praise you. Amen.

Life and Dignity of the Human Person

The Catholic church proclaims that human life is sacred and that the dignity of the human person is the foundation of a moral vision for society. Our belief in the sanctity of human life and the inherent dignity of the human person is the foundation of all the principles of our social teaching. In our society, human life is under direct attack from abortion and assisted suicide. The value of human life is being threatened by increasing use of the death penalty. We believe that every person is precious, that people are more important than things, and that the measure of every institution is whether it threatens or enhances the life and dignity of the human person.

U.S. Conference of Catholic Bishops

The church holds up the inherent dignity of the human person as the foundation and basis for all other social teachings. If we don't respect life, the other teachings have nothing to stand on. This teaching encompasses both the intentional taking of human life and the cold disregard that devalues human life. In *Christifideles Laici*, Pope John Paul II said: "Every violation of the personal dignity of the human being cries out in vengeance to God and is an offense against the Creator" (§37).

Some people interpret the bishops' emphasis on the life and dignity of the human person to refer exclusively to the abortion issue.

Because we use the word "pro-life" to mean anti-abortion in the political arena, we may unconsciously translate the church's pro-life teaching into abortion. But that would be incomplete. When the church talks about the life and dignity of the human person, it means every human person—the elderly, the poor, the condemned, the unborn, the young, the minority, the discouraged, as well as the rich, the powerful, and the strong.

Embracing this teaching takes us up against the reality that we human beings like to separate the world into "us" and "them." We can easily see humanity in those people who we classify as "us," but it's much more difficult to see it in those we classify as "them." Truly, the only way we can be unjust to another human being is to trick ourselves into believing that they're not really human.

The only way a person can get an abortion is by thinking the baby isn't a real person. The only way to kill a murderer is to convince ourselves that in the act of murder, they ceased being human. The only way to tolerate euthanasia is to convince ourselves that the person's humanity is no longer present. The only way that slavery and segregation could be withstood was by tricking ourselves into thinking that blacks weren't truly human. And it's the only way a soldier can get through war, to lose all recognition that "the enemy" is, in fact, a brother or sister.

This teaching on the dignity of the human person is based squarely on Jesus' command to love our neighbor. In the story of the Good Samaritan (Luke 10:29–37), Jesus teaches that loving our neighbor is a command for the one doing the loving, not the one being loved. By living out this teaching in every part of our lives, we truly embrace the gospel and reside in the kingdom of heaven. In the end, living the gospel is all about investing the energy to care.

Living out this first social teaching has three faces: uplifting the dignity of life; resisting those things that degrade life; and expanding our "us" to include the whole world.

Five-minute activities

• *Smile at people who are a different race or ethnicity than you.*
A smile can have a remarkable effect. It is one of the ways we human beings express genuine acceptance. When Mexican immigrants talk about the prejudice they experience, the negative looks people give them are one of the things that pains them the most. The next time you are the one with the opportunity to give a look, make it a smile.

• *Donate to a pregnancy center.*
Pregnancy centers help women deal with the very real pressures that lead to abortion. We, as a society, put many women in the spot of literally deciding between homelessness and abortion; I've known enough pregnant, homeless women to know how true that is. Pregnancy centers are one of the most effective mechanisms for reducing abortion because they make it easier for women to do the right thing. Donate to one in your area, knowing that you are building up life.

• *React with shock whenever somebody says how expensive it is to keep somebody alive.*
Pope John Paul II said: "The value of one person transcends all the material world" (*Christifideles Laici,* §92). One of the sins of our culture is that we tend to base the value of everything, even human life, on money. When somebody complains about how expensive it is to keep somebody alive, simply repeat back what is said with shock in your voice. You might also say something like, "Money is a tool, but life is from God." Remain friendly and welcoming and allow the conversation to continue. You will have made your point, and you may be confident that God will continue the work from there.

• *Join your local Right to Life organization.*
Abortion may be the law of the land, but that doesn't mean we have to accept it. Join an anti-abortion group, such as Right to Life (www.nrlc.org), that works to end abortion in a comprehensive

way—by working to change the law as well as the circumstances that contribute to abortion.

- **Offer heartfelt congratulations every time you hear of a new pregnancy.**

Uplifting human life can be done in small and subtle ways, but these ways are powerful because they contain so much meaning. When you hear that somebody is pregnant, offer heartfelt congratulations. Acknowledge that pregnancy is a new life created by God. Blessings may come with struggles, but they are still blessings.

- **Treat the elderly with respect. Assume they are capable of understanding and making decisions for themselves until proven otherwise.**

When my eighty-year-old grandma (a woman who had worked as a nurse her entire life) was in the hospital, I was shocked when some doctors and nurses treated her like she was incapable of understanding them and making her own decisions. The elderly are not children. While many need help, treating them with basic respect means allowing them self-determination whenever possible.

- **Join Pax Christi.**

Pax Christi is a Catholic organization whose mission is to work for human rights, especially in building up peace in the world. You can learn more and join by visiting www.paxchristi.net.

- **Join Amnesty International.**

Amnesty International works for human rights, especially in campaigns to end the death penalty, to abolish torture, to stop violence against women, to protect the right to food, and to stop weapons proliferation. You can learn more and join by visiting www.amnestyusa.org.

- **Throughout your day, pay attention to people whom you dismiss easily.**

In our daily lives we easily dismiss some people as invisible. They can be secretaries or retail clerks, the homeless on the sidewalk or poor women with several children, or people we never see, like janitors, cooks, or utility workers. Find one person who was invisible to you today and reflect on their genuine humanity.

- *Donate and/or volunteer time at your local food bank.*

The fact that hunger exists in the wealthiest nation on earth is horrifying. Food banks provide immediate and emergency care for families and individuals that literally sustains their lives. Feeding the hungry is truly to care for Christ himself (Matthew 25:40).

- *Join your state's Catholic Conference legislative network.*

When your state's Catholic Conference enters the legislature, it does so standing on the shoulders of thousands and thousands of Catholic citizens around the state. By joining this legislative network, you participate in its work by contacting your legislators at strategic times on important bills.

- *If you have health insurance, use doctors and hospitals that take low-income patients.*

Our current health care system is structured around health insurance, but many hospitals and health care professionals refuse to be bound by this system by treating the uninsured or the underinsured at great financial risk. Make it easier for those who care for these children of God by using their services when you have health insurance, giving them the income to do their life-saving work.

Ten-minute activities

- *Oppose unjust wars.*

At its core, war devalues human life. The military knows that the only way people will kill intentionally is if they are convinced that the enemy is not human. War not only destroys the people killed on the battlefield, it often destroys the lives of those who survive. Assume that every armed conflict is unjust until proven otherwise, and base your opinion on the just war doctrine. Voice your opposition to unjust wars.

- *Write a letter supporting universal health care.*

According to the National Health Insurance Survey (www.cdc.gov/nchs/data/nhis/) conducted by the Center for Disease Control (CDC), 14.4% of the population of the U.S. lived without health insurance in 2005. For these uninsured, universal health care can be the difference between life and death. Write a letter to your congressmen.

- *Write a letter opposing restrictions on welfare based on number of children.*

It has been found that when public support does not cover new children, the rate of abortion among low-income women increases. For example, the abortion rate increased fourteen percent in New Jersey after a family cap was established, according to the *National Catholic Reporter* (9/18/04). If people already are struggling to make ends meet, they hesitate to welcome a new baby who will add to their expenses. Write your legislators.

- *Join an anti-hunger organization.*

Feeding the hungry can mean addressing the immediate care of people oppressed by food injustice. It also mean identifying why hunger exists in the first place, and joining the efforts of others to end hunger. When you work for food justice, you have the potential to feed thousands of families.

- *Actively resist sexism.*

Decades after the women's movement, sexism continues to be pervasive. While much improvement has been made, young boys and young girls are still held to different standards, we still tolerate the widespread under-compensation of women, and we still see leadership as fundamentally a male role. Refuse to be part of the thinking that sees women as less than men. After all, "God created human beings, male and female he created them" (Genesis 1:27).

- *Write your congressmen condemning foreign policy that supports abortion, war, or any kind of killing.*

In our us/them thinking, we tend to focus on the way foreign policy affects us rather than the way it affects our brothers and sisters living in other countries. Oftentimes, our foreign policy is not only oppressive, but it actually encourages killing, as when the people in Guatemala were victimized by the American-backed Sandinistas. Look for the affects of our foreign policies and note your resistance to all policies that devalue human life.

- **Write your legislators in support of prenatal health care for low-income women.**

Imagine that you are caught in an unexpected pregnancy with no support from your husband or boyfriend, and no economic security. Add to this all the messages about how important prenatal care is, but you don't have health insurance. Is it any wonder that many women fall into despair? Advocate for prenatal health care for all women so that nobody has to undergo a pregnancy without health care for herself and her baby.

- **Oppose the death penalty.**

Sit down for ten minutes, and write a letter to your legislators asking them to sponsor a bill to abolish the death penalty. It doesn't have to be long or give eloquent reasons. Just state your opinion, say that you are Catholic, and include your name, address, and phone number. You can send your note by e-mail or regular mail.

- **Teach your children love.**

We teach our children what we truly believe. When we allow our children to call others names, be mean to each other, or embarrass others, we are teaching them that these are acceptable ways of treating other human beings. I'm not suggesting that children simply be forbidden from doing these things; rather, encourage conversations where you help your children to see the destructiveness of those behaviors and urge them to seek reconciliation.

- **Write a letter to the editor opposing the death penalty.**

The public square of our day is the letter to the editor page. Participate in the public conversation by writing a short letter arguing against the death penalty. Keep it to about 150 words.

- **Reflect on the gift of those you love.**

Nowhere is the value and dignity of the human person easier to see than in those you love. Spend some time today reflecting on the gift of their lives. What makes them special? Why is loving them easy? Then take that feeling and consider how God feels about every single human being.

- **Reflect on the gift of someone you despise.**

Sometimes the person we have the most difficulty valuing is not someone on the other side of the planet, but someone we know very well and can't stand: a politician, a co-worker, a mean-spirited parishioner, or a nasty neighbor. Spend some time reflecting on the church's teaching that every person's life has value and dignity. Can you find the value in the life of someone you dislike? If the answer is no, you haven't looked hard enough.

- **Reflect on the gift of your own life.**

Spend a few minutes today reflecting on the gift of your own life. Reflect on your dignity and worth, which is based on nothing more than your creation by the one living God. Do you base your value on other things? If these things were gone, could you still see yourself as a valuable human being? Do you treat your own life as sacred by keeping healthy habits?

- **Does any part of your life participate in the taking of life?**

Some people are more directly involved in the taking of human life than others, but chances are that we all do things to degrade human life. Spend some time recognizing those areas in your life: being apathetic about capital punishment; ignoring the crisis of health insurance coverage; buying food without regard for the people who grew it; disregarding the struggles of people facing crisis pregnancies.

- **Develop empathy for one new person or group of people.**

The first step in really supporting life and respecting the dignity of all is to see people as "us" rather than "them." Today, recall one person you regard as "them," somebody in a different socio-economic class or with different politics or of a different race. Think about that one person today—what he or she is doing, what he or she wants out of life, the struggles in his or her life, and the struggles that formed his or her life.

Twenty-minute activities

• *Learn about the just war doctrine.*

Opposing unjust wars begins with understanding the difference between a just war and an unjust war. Visit the U.S. Bishop's Web site at www.usccb.org, and search for "just war." A good synopsis of this doctrine is found at www.usccb.org/sdwp/international/just-war.htm. The church has many statements and documents that further explain this vital church teaching.

• *Tell your children stories about when their grandparents and great-grandparents were young.*

Tell your children stories and examples that reveal the humanity of their grandparents. Choose stories that will make sense to children and help them see their grandparents as real people who were very much like them.

• *Write a letter to your legislator asking them to sponsor a bill that eliminates all social and legal causes of abortion.*

Right now abortion is a constitutional right, but that doesn't mean it cannot be dealt with effectively in law. Challenge your congressmen to find a solution to abortion, including eliminating the very real reasons that lead people to abortion. (You could ask them to call the bill, "Making It Easy to Value Life Bill.")

• *Execute a death penalty living will.*

Write up a statement that if you are murdered, you do not want your murderer to be sentenced to death. Sign and date it with a notary public (usually banks, diocesan offices, and local government offices have someone on staff who is a notary public), and keep it with your will.

- **Join the March for Life.**

Every January in cities all over the country, people march on the anniversary of *Roe v. Wade*. It is a demonstration against the legalization of abortion, and it is typically a forum where people from many different faiths and backgrounds gather around their common love for life. Contact your diocesan pro-life ministry to find out the specifics for your area.

- **Examine your own assumptions about blacks or Hispanics or Jews or Asians or whites.**

Racism is an ugly part of the human experience. Judging people as less based on their race is a systemic way of refusing to see one's dignity and value as a human being. But chances are that even those who think of themselves as liberated from prejudice still carry some subtle and latent "them" thinking. This often reveals itself in fear, in assumptions about intelligence or education, and in an apathetic response to unjust living conditions. Spend twenty minutes today searching your soul honestly.

- **Advocate for paid maternity leave at your company.**

Offering economic security to people at this time is a basic kindness consistent with the love and mercy of God. Express your support for offering this type of benefit to employees at your company.

- **Reflect on those things that uplift life.**

If the dignity of life was upheld universally, what would that look like? Spend twenty minutes today thinking about what uplifting life means. What does that truly mean in your life and in the community?

- **Write a letter to someone on death row.**

E-mail your diocesan prison ministry and ask how you can become a pen pal to someone on death row. A letter can make a real difference to a person who has been told by their government that his or her life is so worthless it will be terminated.

- **If you have been involved in the taking of human life, make a heartfelt confession and experience the peace of reconciliation.**

Forgiving oneself for the taking of life is probably one of the most difficult things a person must do. This is the living nightmare of the soldier, the post-abortive woman, the murderer, the prosecutor who won a death penalty conviction, or the people who pressured those decisions. The very act of feeling sorrow and regret is, in fact, accepting the mercy of God. Receive the sacrament of reconciliation, and seek peace with God and the church.

- **Reflect on the institutions you are a part of and how they either threaten or enhance the life and dignity of the human person.**

We each belong to many different institutions operating in our world: city, county, state, and federal governments; church; voluntary organizations; political parties; professional organizations; and so forth. Select one institution that you are part of and reflect on how this institution raises up life, or on how it degrades human dignity.

- **Execute a living will.**

Living wills are ways that people of all ages can communicate their wishes when they are unable to speak for themselves. They are a mechanism for participating as a valuable human being in your own decisions. Call your local hospital and get some information about living wills.

- **Learn about the people who get abortions.**

Visit the Web site for the Center for Disease Control's abortion statistics at www.cdc.gov/reproductivehealth/surv_abort.htm to find out more about the people who get abortions. You might be surprised that in 2000, eighty percent of abortions were performed on women who were twenty years of age and older. More abortions are done on women who already have at least one child than on first-time mothers. Many abortions are done on married women. Call your diocesan pro-life ministry or visit the National Right to Life Committee Web site at www.nrlc.org to find out some of the reasons women get abortions. Understanding this issue from the perspective of the women themselves helps us follow God's call to make a difference in the reality of abortion.

• Learn about the people in your area who are on death row.
Contact your state Catholic Conference or the American Civil
Liberties Union to find out more about the death row inmates in
your state. But don't just stop with learning about those on death
row; learn about others who have committed similar crimes and
what happened to them. You might be surprised to discover that
the death penalty is usually given to the poor. According to
Gardner Hanks in *Against the Death Penalty*, about ninety percent
of those condemned to death could not afford their own attorney.

Call to Family, Community, and Participation

The person is not only sacred but also social. How we organize our society in economics and politics, in law and policy directly affects human dignity and the capacity of individuals to grow in community. The family is the central social institution that must be supported and strengthened, not undermined. We believe people have a right and a duty to participate in society, seeking together the common good and well-being of all, especially the poor and vulnerable.

U.S. Conference of Catholic Bishops

One of the worst things that can happen to a person is to lose their ability to participate in a community. Participating in family and community gives meaning to our lives. Participation is so important that children who grow up without connection to others are permanently handicapped; criminals put in solitary confinement often lose their sanity.

People need other people to be human. The genius of the Catholic Worker movement is that, rather than just caring for the homeless, they are empowered to participate. This opportunity to participate gives the homeless the strength to do the demanding and difficult work of getting off the streets.

The call to participation broadly addresses all the different ways we relate to other people, that is, our family, neighborhood, socio-economic class, and government. It defines the ways we organize ourselves. Rather than assuming that every structure and institution is divinely ordained, however, structures need to be examined, because sin and grace co-exist in every institution and organization.

Learning about Catholic social teaching might seem like an opportunity to judge others but it is not so. It is easy to hear this call and instead of using it to illuminate areas for pastoral growth, all that is seen is the error of others. Jesus did not tell us to wait around for the rest of the world to be perfect before living the gospel. We, the followers of Jesus, are to be the leaven in the dough, the light in the darkness, and the salt to flavor the world. We're the ones who show the rest of the world what can be done. We are called to personally live out these teachings, and make it easy for others to do so.

It's not sufficient to just participate, however; our participation must be grounded in the common good. Adolf Hitler, Al Capone, and Ken Lay participated in their communities, but they weren't committed to the common good. While most people are not quite so criminal, the truth is that we all have room for growth in turning our attention toward the common good.

Five-minute activities

• *Vote.*

There is no more basic and important way of participating in our society than to vote. I have heard a lot of excuses from people for not voting, and they all seem to be based in apathy rather than love of community. Even if you think it won't make one bit of difference to the world, vote anyway. It makes a big difference to who you are as a human being.

- *Learn your neighbor's names.*

Our neighborhoods are becoming less and less neighborly. Most people would love to be friendly with their neighbors, but they just don't know how to get started. The next time you see a neighbor, walk over, introduce yourself, and ask their name.

- *Smile at families in church.*

For many parents, just getting the children to church can be exhausting. When you see families at church, especially those with high-spirited children, smile at them. Participating in community includes many different levels of connections to people, and smiles build connections.

- *Sit outside or on the front step in nice weather.*

It's easy to remain separate from your neighbors with all the comforts inside the home, but just spending some time outside makes you available to your neighbors in a way that builds trust and safety.

- *Support and encourage your child's relationship with both parents.*

Somewhere along the line, we seem to have decided that mothers are the real parents, and fathers are just helpers. Take an active part in raising your children, regardless of your gender. Provide space and support for your spouse to parent, as well. If you are divorced, support a strong relationship between your children and their other parent.

- *Embrace your role as a parent.*

Our culture proclaims that spending money on toys, vacations, clothes, cars, education, and so on is a big part of being a good parent. The truth is that being a good parent simply means taking care of your children, providing for their upbringing, and guiding them. But that simplicity is loaded with responsibility. Children need your strength, protection, love, and endurance to grow into the people God created them to be.

- *Notice if the policies in your workplace support or degrade family life.*

Some employers are damaging to family life by demanding long or irregular hours. Pay attention to the policies at your work. If they support family life, then follow that support by investing yourself into your family life. If they degrade family life, offer subtle but consistent resistance.

• *Join your state's Catholic Conference legislative network.*

Your state's Catholic Conference works on bills that uplift family life, and they need your help to be successful. By joining their legislative network, you can participate in their work by contacting your legislators at crucial times on important bills. Visit www.nasccd.org to find your state's Catholic Conference.

• *Join the neighborhood association.*

Neighborhood associations are a powerful way of participating in neighborhood life. Joining one is a good way to come to know your neighbors, as well as help contribute toward a healthy neighborhood.

Ten-minute activities

• *Write down five things that make good parenting easier.*

There are a million things that call us away from our fundamental responsibility as parents, and resisting them can be more than one can bear. Smile at people when they are doing the hard work of parenting. Comment on the beauty of their children so they can see it. Create situations where children can be themselves, making them feel welcome and allowing their parents to relax. Write down five things you can do to make it easier for others to be good parents.

• *Find out if there is a place for homeless families in your community.*

Many communities have homeless shelters for single men or women with children, but intact families are often the last to be provided for. Homelessness is hard enough without ripping families apart. Call city hall and find out what is available in your community.

• *Join something.*

In the last fifty years, our society has become more and more fractured as people move away from group activities and toward individual ones. Having fun with others builds strong bonds that transcend the things that keep us apart. Pick something to join—a bowling league, a book club, a play group, a Bible study, anything that requires your physical presence and participation.

• Reflect on spending as participation.

In our culture, buying can feel like a more basic exercise of citizenship than voting. Being grounded in Catholic social teaching means that we consider our own spending. Reflect on the extent to which you use spending as participation.

• Join a babysitting co-op.

Babysitting co-ops are citizen-run organizations where people trade babysitting within the group. In addition to having access to babysitting services, you'll have the opportunity to reach out to the community.

• Give your hand-me-downs to a struggling family.

Feeling like you are part of something can be more difficult when you are struggling financially. By offering (or accepting) hand-me-downs, you are both helping out another family and building a connection with them.

• Reflect on education for job skills or citizenship.

Education prepares children for adult life. Tension has existed for a long time between the idea that education should be primarily about preparing citizens to participate in their communities or about preparing workers for jobs. Reflect for ten minutes on the differences between the two approaches, and note your own conclusions.

• Think back to the last political statement you made; does your position further the common good?

Think back to the last time you voiced an opinion about a political issue. Who benefits from your position? How does it serve the common good? Could another position better serve the common good? Reflect on your answers, and see if your opinion changes.

• Join a living wage coalition.

Meaningful participation is difficult when you are working three jobs just to make ends meet. When people work full-time and still don't have enough money to meet their basic needs, their human dignity is violated and their ability to participate in their community is restrained. Join a coalition that supports a living wage being paid to all workers. Visit www.livingwage.org for ideas.

- *Examine the way you and your family spend time; is it the best way to build family life?*

Spend ten minutes today reflecting back on the last week. Write down what you did during the time you spent together as a family. Think critically about whether the way you spent your time together was the best way to build family life. What changes could you make to improve family life? What aspects are working well and need to be protected?

- *Reflect on the life of a poor or oppressed person; how are they denied participation in the community? in society as a whole?*

Truly seeing the perspective of another is very difficult for humans because we are locked into our own viewpoints. Spend ten minutes reflecting on the life of a poor or oppressed person, and identify specific ways they are denied participation.

- *Reflect on those parts of your life where you resist participation.*

Resisting participation is a mechanism for avoiding responsibility to family or community. Reflect on the ways you resist participation, even hiding the responsibility from yourself. Shed light on those things you keep in the dark, and invite God into that darkness.

- *Reflect on why each person should participate in their family and community.*

Why is participation so important? What does it have to do with the kingdom of heaven and the good news? Why is it important for human beings? Give yourself permission to stop the reflection after ten minutes.

- *Reflect on what is meant by "common good."*

Words can be difficult because they often mean different things to different people. What do *you* mean when you think of "common good"? Write down your definition, then see if you can find support for your definition in the gospels.

• *Work on your own marriage.*

The call to be family is a call to build and sustain relationships. For most people, marriage is their foundational relationship. Spend ten minutes reflecting on the importance of your marriage and the ways you could nurture it, or spend ten minutes having this discussion with your spouse. What aspects of your marriage are life-giving and wonderful, and what aspects need some nurturing?

Twenty-minute activities

• *Attend a PTA meeting.*

School meetings have become the last vestige of town hall gatherings in an increasingly fractured society. Attending a PTA meeting at your children's school gets you involved in the school and, by extension, in the community at large.

• *Schedule blocks of time to simply be with your family and accomplish nothing.*

We are a people obsessed with accomplishment, so simply spending time together can be very difficult for some. Schedule some time this week to just be with your family, renewing relationships and embracing your own sense of being home. As my daughter says in her little three-year-old voice, "We need time wiff woo."

• *If you are denied participation, are you resisting or cooperating with that denial?*

Chances are that almost all of us are denied participation at times; exclusion is the nature of social sin. When this happens, how do we respond? Do we cooperate or resist? Jesus gave us a model of how to actively resist sin when he was questioned before the Sanhedrin.

• *Envision a parish community in which all participate.*

We can be so stuck in the way our world works today that we lose the ability to imagine what the world would be like without sin. Spend twenty minutes today imagining a community in which all participate. Write down your vision. This exercise requires that you find eyes to see the people who may now be invisible.

• **Reflect on the role of your own family in your life.**

Our family should be central to our life. Yet in the business of life, we can end up rushing through life without connecting to those who give us meaning. Spend twenty minutes journaling about the role of your family in your life.

• **Make a date with a friend.**

The importance of friendship is unquestionable to a healthy and happy life. But friendships take time and energy to develop and to maintain; they also take risk and courage in the revelation of self. Take the risk, make the connection, and work to sustain those important relationships. This week find a way to spend twenty minutes with a friend.

• **Spend some time reflecting on how the poor can both be cared for and given the ability to participate at the same time.**

We live with a tension in our society between the idea that the poor need to be cared for, and the idea that the poor need to be empowered to make their own lives better. How can we provide a safety net to catch people when they are falling but at the same time allow them freedom and dignity?

• **Volunteer in a political campaign.**

As we have become less and less communal, we tend to see money as the primary resource in elections—rather than volunteers. The truth is that volunteers are still the most important component to a successful political campaign. By joining a campaign, you are participating in your community in a real and effective way. Find a candidate who you believe in and get involved.

• **Go to the library.**

The library provides an easy way to participate and be in the community. Not only are libraries open to all people, but also they tend to be places of gathering and community posting. Take a twenty-minute trip to the library; just browse or look for other ways to participate in your community.

- *Reflect on how our economy excludes some people from participation.*

Every economic system places some people on the inside, and some people on the outside. How does our own economy exclude people? Reflect on who is excluded, in what ways. Don't try to solve the problem in this twenty minutes; just be aware that it exists.

- *Envision a world that uplifts family life.*

What would a world that uplifts family life look like? Be specific. How would it be the same as today's world? How would it be different? Draw a picture.

- *Reflect on the organization of society.*

Think about the way society is organized. How could it be organized differently? Spend twenty minutes writing down the ideas that come easily. Then come back tomorrow and spend twenty minutes trying to envision more. Enjoy the sight you have discovered.

- *Attend a candidate forum at election time.*

Voting is important, and so is making informed decisions. During campaign season, attend a candidate forum. You'll learn more about the candidates, and you'll also learn more about the people in your own community.

- *Join a parish committee.*

Participate in your parish community by picking one aspect of parish life that excites you, and join (or start) a committee.

- *Volunteer to watch children while their parents are at a Marriage Encounter.*

Parents of young children must care for their children constantly, and many do not have the option of taking the weekend off to work on their marriage. Make it easy for them to invest in their marriage by taking their children for the weekend. Even better, coordinate this at your parish, matching up couples with people who would watch their children.

Rights and Responsibilities

The Catholic tradition teaches that human dignity can be pro-tected and a healthy community can be achieved only if human rights are protected and responsibilities are met. Therefore, every person has a fundamental right to life and a right to those things required for human decency. Corresponding to these rights are duties and responsibilities to one another, to our families, and to the larger society.

U.S. Conference of Catholic Bishops

In our political arena, liberals traditionally focus on rights and conservatives traditionally focus on responsibilities. The church teaches that these are two sides of the same coin. They go together and only by uplifting both do we follow the gospel.

Many will argue that a person only has rights if they meet their responsibilities, and they quote St. Paul out of context: "anyone unwilling to work should not eat" (2 Thessalonians 3:10). The church rejects this notion. Our right to food is not dependent on whether or not we live out our responsibilities. Otherwise, it wouldn't be a right; it would be a privilege. Rights are those things that are endowed by the Creator. The unborn baby's right to life doesn't stem from their current or future responsibilities; their right to life is fundamental and permanent.

But if we neglect our responsibilities, our commitment to rights is shallow and limp. Your right to live free of racism is dependent on my treating you fairly. My right to freedom of religion is dependent on you not forcing your religion, or lack thereof, on me. My neighbor's children's right to education is dependent on my contribution toward the schools. Recognizing that the rights of others originate from God is lived out in our responsibility toward one another.

When we look at the way we actually live our lives, we find that we already embrace these concepts in our everyday activities. I have parental rights as a mother to my children, and I also have the responsibility to care for and parent them. We have the right to vote as citizens, and we therefore carry the responsibility for the actions of our government.

In this teaching the church articulates the basic human rights: the right to food, shelter, clothing, health care, education, freedom of religion and expression, establishing a family, and life. Charity steps in where justice has failed. For example, even though health care is a commodity-based system, emergency rooms often don't turn away people who are dying because of inability to pay.

Living out this teaching includes both upholding rights and living out responsibilities, especially those responsibilities that flesh out human rights. Because our political climate is polarized on this issue, for some people spiritual growth will occur as their eyes are opened to the nature of human rights. For others, spiritual growth will occur by recognizing personal and communal responsibilities. Discomfort can help you find your growth edge.

Five-minute activities

• *Donate to a health center.*
For the millions of people living without health insurance or sufficient health insurance, exercising their right to health can be fraught with complications and rejection. Health centers provide

life-giving medical care to people who can't afford to use the mainstream system. Support their work by making a donation.

- **Give diapers to the food bank.**

Diapers are an expensive and ongoing part of caring for a baby, and for many of the people coming into the food bank, this expense is more than they can bear. Donate a package of diapers to ease the burden of these people.

- **Live in an integrated neighborhood.**

As we strive to overcome racism, our success or failure is most apparent in the places we live. Remind yourself what you lose when you live without diversity. Welcome people from other races into your neighborhood, and the next time you move, opt for an integrated neighborhood.

- **Vote.**

Voting is one of our primary rights and responsibilities. It seems unbelievable that half of all women, who received the right to vote less than a century ago, now give up that right voluntarily. Take your responsibility seriously. Vote. Do it for the common good.

- **Donate to an inner city community center.**

The historic beating hearts of urban centers have become today's abandoned inner cities, mired in poverty. When the things that sustain human life, such as meaningful work, decent living conditions, and connections to community, break down, crime and violence increase. In many inner cities, people have come together to rebuild their communities. Support their work by making a donation to an organization that is active in inner city work.

- **Shop in an urban area that is struggling.**

People who live in poor urban areas need things like grocery and drug stores nearby to exercise their right to buy food. But maintaining a store in a struggling area can be an uphill battle. Notice stores in struggling areas and shop there once in a while.

- **Join Habitat for Humanity.**

The dream of home ownership, especially a decent house, is out of reach for many of our brothers and sisters. Habitat for Humanity helps to make that dream a reality. Donate to the organization or support their work by becoming a volunteer.

- **Donate to a food bank.**

Sustenance is a fundamental human right, but many suffer from hunger in this nation of abundance. Share that abundance with the children of God by donating to your parish or city food bank.

- **Watch out for your neighbors.**

Something as simple as being aware of your neighbors and just noticing them is a way of living out your responsibility to others. You may notice someone struggling with issues of food, security, racism, or unemployment. You can offer comfort and possibly help.

- **Pray in thanksgiving at tax time.**

Income tax is one of the ways that we contribute to the larger society. Tax monies support social programs for education and care for the poor, and infrastructures such as police and fire departments, roads, and care for those around the world. Resist the cultural norm of complaining about taxes; instead, pray in thanksgiving for the opportunity to live out your responsibility to the larger society.

- **Join a neighborhood watch.**

It's easy to be part of a neighborhood watch. If you notice something criminal at your neighbor's house, you call the police. It's simple, takes almost no time, and creates a real sense of security for all in the neighborhood.

- **Pay women and minorities the same as white men.**

As our society struggles with pervasive racism and sexism, women still lag behind in wages, and are paid less than men for the same work. (I suspect those wage decisions are made by people who don't think of themselves as sexist.) If you make decisions about wages, notice your practices, and reject any difference between the compensation of men and women or between races. You will make enormous progress in human rights by your actions.

• Take care of your children.

Saying "Take care of your children" may seem obvious, but we have come up with elaborate ways of tricking ourselves out of parental responsibility. Education has become the responsibility of the school. Many quietly abdicate the moral formation of their children to the media. Participation in the church community has too often become the choice of the child rather than the expectation of the parent. Your children depend on you for their upbringing and formation. Live out that responsibility by being involved in your children's lives, and you will be rewarded with joy and meaning.

Ten-minute activities

• Write a letter supporting low-income housing.

Many people are unable to exercise their right to decent housing because of their poverty. Write a letter to the mayor and/or city council voicing your support for public funds to go into low-income housing.

• Use your gifts for the community.

God has gifted each person with unique and individual gifts. Some gifts, like wealth or education, are easy to see, but others are more intrinsic. Some have the gift of music, others the gift of hospitality, others the gift of leadership. Discern your own gifts, and find a way to share them with the community. The Catherine of Siena Institute offers Called & Gifted Workshops to help people discern their gifts. Learn more at www.siena.org.

• Write a letter supporting universal prenatal medical care.

The right to life for the unborn includes the right to decent health care. For those living without maternity coverage or health insurance, their baby's right to life and health is being systematically denied. Write your legislators with your support for universal prenatal medical care.

- **Write a letter supporting urban renewal.**

In the spirit of conservation and the rights of inner city dwellers to decent living conditions, write a letter supporting urban renewal. Rather than abandoning city centers, suggest they be reborn as seats of personal and communal living.

- **Express shock at any racist remark.**

Jokes and remarks that demean African-Americans, Hispanics, Jews, Arabs, or other ethnic and racial groups are still around, and people still laugh at them. Next time this happens in your presence, slowly repeat the words with shock in your voice. Deliver the message that you disapprove, and help others hear the words in a new way.

- **Speak out in support of human rights.**

Martin Luther King, Jr. Day offers the opportunity to reflect and speak out in support of human rights. Join a human rights march. Write a letter to the editor in support of human rights. Do something to use your voice.

- **Write your congressmen to support legislation that heals past human rights abuses.**

Some human rights abuses have been so outrageous and long-lasting that their effects go on for generations, even after the abuse ends. The legacy of slavery and segregation is still real for African-Americans today. Write to your congressmen supporting legislation that heals those past abuses, not because people today caused the problem, but because people today are still being hurt by the effects. Trust that by your efforts, God will heal the hurt and those who did the hurting.

- **Write a letter to the editor opposing assisted suicide.**

Assisted suicide is a misunderstanding and rejection of a person's value and humanity. Write a letter to the editor about the preciousness of life, regardless of age or health.

- **Use your voice to be an advocate for education.**

Being an advocate for education begins with placing priority on the child's right to education over the system they are part of. It can be as simple as writing a letter to the school board regarding an issue you have noticed, or it can be as involved as volunteering regularly to tutor.

• *Are there human rights abuses in your own community?*

Seeing the human rights abuses in the past or in other places is easy. We have much more difficulty seeing the abuses that are happening here right now. You cannot stand up for human rights if you don't see them. Pray for eyes to see.

• *Reflect on what "human rights" means.*

Spend ten minutes reflecting on what "human rights" means to you. What is included? What makes them rights? What are the implications? Write down your ideas.

• *Write the mayor's office in support of services for the homeless.*

Homelessness seems to be one of the dirty little secrets we carry around in our society; we don't want to believe it really happens, so we put enormous distance between ourselves and the people living that way. Write a letter to the mayor saying that you support services and housing for the homeless rather than just moving them away, as some cities do.

• *Reflect on generosity as a responsibility.*

When we contribute to the giving tree, donate to the food bank, or even let a person go ahead of us in line, we feel the warm flush of generosity. The problem is that most of us treat generosity as something above and beyond our everyday actions, rather than a normal part of our responsibility. Reflect for ten minutes on the notion of generosity as responsibility.

• *Write a letter supporting the freedom of hospital and medical personnel to refuse to participate in abortions.*

For most of us the abortion issue is more of an idea than a reality. But for doctors and nurses in hospitals, it can be a very real and daily issue. Write a letter to your congressmen supporting the right of medical personnel and institutions (like Catholic hospitals) to follow their consciences when deciding whether or not to perform abortions.

Twenty-minute activities

• *Watch over children who are not your own.*

Being responsible for one another means that our concern doesn't apply to only our own children. Other children rely on us as well. Protect and comfort children who are not your own. Volunteer to watch them while their parents spend some time alone. Volunteer to be a catechist in your parish.

• *If you're bilingual, volunteer to act as a translator for people caught in the criminal justice system.*

The right to just and fair treatment for those who are caught in the criminal justice system is often difficult due to language barriers. If you're bilingual, volunteer some time to offer translation services. Help those charged with a crime to understand what the charge is and fully explain their story.

• *Learn about the welfare system in your state.*

Learn about the way welfare is administered in your state. Are the rights of the poor protected? If you find any violations of rights, write them down.

• *Join a march for human rights.*

When people are marching for human rights in your town, join the march. Many people are afraid of going to marches, perhaps because they fear being branded as extremists. Invite a friend or bring your family and just walk along; you don't have to do anything more. Your physical presence makes a difference.

• *Reflect on your own human rights.*

The church has a broader understanding of human rights than our culture. Spend twenty minutes reflecting on your own human rights. Are they fully supported by the community around you? Do you exercise your rights? Do you think that any rights are earned rather than being endowed by God?

• *What are your responsibilities?*

Write down all the things you are responsible for. Then write another list of things other people say, or might say, that you are responsible for—with which you don't agree. Go through your lists, taking a few moments to reflect on each item. Are these truly your responsibilities? Do you own them? A few items on both lists probably don't belong there.

• Donate blood.

The ancient Israelites believed that the life force of a person or animal was its blood, making the words of Jesus, "this is my blood," that much more powerful. We may not see blood as a life force, but it certainly contributes to the lives of people in a real way. Go to an American Red Cross center and donate blood.

• Learn about the causes of homelessness and how human rights are being violated.

Learn about the causes of homelessness in your community. How is the right to decent shelter compromised? Where are the weak links in the chain? Remember that oftentimes rights are violated not by evil people, but by good people caught in broken systems.

• What comes first—rights or responsibilities?

Spend twenty minutes reflecting on the relationship between rights and responsibilities. Do you believe that responsibilities must be met before rights can be exercised? Do you believe people have responsibilities to each other? Spend this time getting to better know yourself and your beliefs.

• Get on the bone marrow registry.

Contact your local hospital to find out how to get on the bone marrow registry. If a match is found, your bone marrow could be a contribution that saves another life. If the opportunity to make a donation arises, give your marrow as a gift, freely given in responsibility to another.

• What are the subtle things you do to undermine human rights?

Spend twenty minutes reflecting on your own thinking, attitudes, and behaviors. Does anything in your own life undermine the human rights of others or yourself? This is a very difficult exercise, an examination of conscience that demands we let go of our own defense mechanisms. If you are able to identify an area, mention it the next time you celebrate the sacrament of reconciliation, and feel the surge of forgiveness flow over you.

- **Examine your own sexist thinking.**

Sexism is such a pervasive and subconscious part of our thinking that we can easily be blind to it. Spend twenty minutes thinking about any of your attitudes that view women as less important. The goal here is not to correct the sexist thinking, but just to be aware of it. What things do women do that you consider beneath men? What things that are typically done by men seem unfit for women? This is not an exercise for men only; women can be just as locked into sexist thinking as men.

- **Be active in the political process year-round.**

Political races are often built around the issues that someone else chooses. Only by becoming active in your political party are you able to participate in developing the questions, rather than just reacting to the answers.

- **Volunteer at a hospital.**

When my grandma was in the hospital and not very capable of communicating, my aunt and myself were her advocates. I wondered about the people in the rooms around her. Did they have advocates? Call the chaplaincy office and volunteer to be a voice for those who have lost theirs.

Option for the Poor and Vulnerable

A basic moral test is how our most vulnerable members are faring. In a society marred by deepening divisions between rich and poor, our tradition recalls the story of the Last Judgment (Matthew 25:31–46) and instructs us to put the needs of the poor and vulnerable first.

U.S. Conference of Catholic Bishops

The church puts primacy on the consistent threads that run throughout all of Scripture. One of those threads is care for the poor and vulnerable. God's special care for the poor is apparent throughout the Hebrew Scriptures. "Open your hand to the poor and needy neighbor in your land" (Deuteronomy 15:11). "Do not rob the poor because they are poor, or crush the afflicted at the gate; for the Lord pleads their cause and despoils of life those who despoil them" (Proverbs 22:22). "For he stands at the right hand of the needy, to save them from those who would condemn them to death" (Psalms 109:31). "Sing to the Lord; praise the Lord! For he has delivered the life of the needy from the hands of evildoers" (Jeremiah 20:13). "Do not turn your face away from anyone who is poor, and the face of God will not be turned away from you" (Tobit 4:7).

Jesus put emphasis on care for the poor, as summed up in Matthew's gospel about the last judgment. "Just as you did it to one of the least of these who are members of my family, you did it to me" (Matthew 25:40). The other gospels record the same focus: Mark's story of the rich young man ends with the words, "It is easier for a camel to go through the eye of a needle than for someone who is rich to enter the kingdom of god" (Mark 10:25). This same theme is present in Luke's story of the Rich Man and Lazarus (Luke 16:19–31).

The preferential place of the poor and vulnerable makes complete sense when you think from God's perspective. The wealthy and the strong are able to care for themselves and defend themselves. But the poor and the vulnerable lack the voice, the strength, or the resources to defend themselves. God stands on their behalf, and any attack against them is an attack against God. This principle is simple, clear—and challenging!

Being God's partner in speaking up for the poor and the vulnerable demands that we see with the eyes of God: that we use our strength to defend, that we see the poor and vulnerable as peers rather than inferiors, and that we squarely move away from any and all oppression of the poor.

Five-minute activities

• **Donate to a food bank.**
Feeding the hungry is one of the corporal works of mercy. It is one of the most fundamental charitable actions to which we are called. Find a food bank in your parish or your city, and make a donation.

• **Donate school supplies or coats to a school in an inner city or rural area.**
Poor families struggle to provide the most basic supplies for their children. Identify the poorest school district in your state or in your city, and make a donation. School supplies are needed most early in the school year. During the winter, coats and boots (for those of us in the colder climates) are always needed.

- *Smile at people who appear poor and look them in the eye.*

We value self-sufficiency in the United States and by definition, poverty is the lack of self-sufficiency. Most of us have a gut-level fear of poverty, and so we avert our eyes when we are faced with it. But poor people are still people, created in the image and likeness of God. Put your love of humanity above your fear and look people who are poor in the eye. Smile at them.

- *Donate to a music scholarship fund for low-income kids.*

Music continues to be treated as superfluous in many places. As a result, instruments and lessons are often only available for the well-to-do. Donate to a music scholarship fund that helps low-income kids take music lessons and obtain instruments. Call your school district to find one. If a scholarship doesn't exist, start one.

- *In your own mind, measure welfare reform by a reduction in poverty rather than a reduction in public roles.*

Welfare reform has many people excited about fewer people on the public roles; but the actual poverty rate hasn't changed much. Although many problems exist with welfare, simply reforming the system to reduce the number of people receiving assistance is not the answer. Take notice of the poverty rate when you see it and note your own conclusions.

- *Donate to Catholic Charities.*

Catholic Charities works on the root causes of poverty and dysfunction, and provides invaluable services to people all over the country. Contact your diocesan Catholic Charities agency and make a donation, or visit www.catholiccharitiesinfo.org to find your local agency.

- *Shop in second-hand stores and in poor neighborhoods.*

Putting the poor and vulnerable first includes raising your awareness of the lives of the poor. By shopping where they shop, you receive insight into their lives as well as support the businesses serving them.

- *Catch yourself when you blame the poor for their poverty.*

We often carry around the idea that there are "deserving poor" and the "undeserving poor." This comes from blaming the poor for their poverty. How similar we are to the disciples who asked Jesus: "Who sinned, this man or his parents, that he was born blind?" (John 9:2). Even when we have been converted to Jesus' way of seeing, we can be subconsciously sucked into our culture's attitudes. If you catch yourself blaming the poor for their condition, notice it and rejoice that you caught youself.

• *Join the Society of St. Vincent de Paul.*

The Society of St. Vincent de Paul is a parish-based organization of people working to help the real problems of the poor. In addition to running food banks, members of the Society of St. Vincent de Paul assist in areas such as help with housing, heating bills, and legal services. Participate in their work in whatever capacity you can.

• *Avoid buying from companies that create or maintain poverty with their wages or business practices.*

Notice newspaper stories about companies that fail to pay a living wage or treat their workers justly. Avoid shopping at these stores or purchasing products from those companies. You can investigate companies in your area by visiting www.responsibleshopper.org, a Web site that maintains a directory of major companies and their business practices.

• *Be mindful that your weekly offering affects the wages of church workers.*

Our church continues to struggle with paying a living wage to those who invest their full-time efforts in ministry. Be mindful that part of the struggle is based on parish collections. When you make your offering, be aware of the effect it has on the wages of church workers.

• *Look for the invisible poor.*

We can easily spot a homeless person on the street or in the park, but thousands more remain invisible. These are the working poor who hold down two or three jobs to make ends meet, and the farmers who struggle to maintain a way of life. Look for the invisible poor in your community.

• *Pray for the poor, and always include "we."*

Prayer is a powerful and significant part of living out Catholic social teaching, but be careful that you aren't praying to a "Santa Claus god" who solves all problems with magic. When we pray for the poor, our prayer should always include "we": *Lord, watch over those suffering from poverty, that we may see their need and respond with generosity and justice. Amen.*

Ten-minute activities

• *Write a letter to support increasing the minimum wage.*

In 1968, the minimum wage was $1.60 per hour; that's $8.46 in 2003 dollars. By 2004 the federal minimum wage was $5.15 per hour, far less than what is needed for a basic living wage. Raising the minimum wage is one significant step toward justice for the poor. Write your congressmen with your support for increasing the federal and/or state minimum wage.

• *Write a letter in support of protecting the rights of immigrants.*

"You shall not deprive a resident alien or an orphan of justice" (Deuteronomy 24:17). People have a long history of emigrating for a better life. The ancient Hebrews did it when they left Egypt; Joseph and Mary did it when they fled Herod's extermination of male Jewish babies. Our church holds that people have a right to emigrate, especially when they are fleeing poverty or persecution. Write a letter to your legislators supporting fair treatment for immigrants.

• *Join a living-wage coalition.*

Payment of a living wage has become one of the basic justice issues around poverty. Find a living-wage coalition and join with others to end the scandal of people who work full-time and still live in poverty. Many cities and states have living-wage coalitions. Visit www.livingwagecampaign.org for more information.

• **Write to city hall supporting drug and alcohol rehabilitation programs.**

In my hometown, the two major problems that keep people in homelessness are mental illness and addiction, but there are few programs available to help people get off drugs or alcohol. Write to your mayor and/or city council supporting investment in drug and alcohol rehabilitation facilities in your city. Help the homeless, along with countless others who are possessed by the demon of addiction.

• **Look at how you glean your own fields.**

"When you reap the harvest of your land, you shall not reap to the very edges of your field, or gather the gleanings of your harvest...you shall leave them for the poor and the alien" (Leviticus 19:9–10). For those of us who aren't farmers, this command requires reflection. Spend ten minutes thinking about how it applies to your life.

• **Take one public policy and view it from the perspective of someone who is poor.**

If you are not suffering from poverty, you can easily miss the way public policies affect the poor. Pick one public policy and spend ten minutes understanding its affect on the poor. What are its benefits and what are its dark sides? During this reflection, move your consciousness to the perspective of the poor.

• **Write to city hall opposing ordinances that chase the homeless out of town.**

Rather than addressing homelessness, many cities attack the homeless. There are ordinances against loitering, sleeping in the park, and panhandling. Some cities will even pay for one-way bus tickets out of town. Write to the mayor and/or city council opposing all ordinances that chase the homeless away, challenging them instead to work on eliminating homelessness in your town.

• **For one week, live on what a family at the poverty level is able to afford.**

Preferential care for the poor can easily become paternalistic for those who don't suffer from poverty. As a spiritual exercise, live on the grocery budget of a family living at the poverty level. Visit www.usda.gov and search for "household food security." Calculate the weekly budget for your family at the "Thrifty Food Plan" level and then live on it. Remember, this pertains to all food, not just groceries, so include school lunch, eating out, and so forth.

- *Write a letter supporting health care for low-income people.*

Even buying into employer-provided health care is more than some people are able to do. Write a letter to your legislators and congressmen supporting an investment into health care for low-income people. Tell them that you would like to see health care for low-income people rise to the same quality and availability given to those on standard health insurance plans.

- *Don't buy something; resist the materialism that breeds disdain for the poor.*

Greed, also known as "materialism," and disdain for the poor go hand in hand. Make a conscious choice not to buy something that you don't need. The poor do this all the time, but involuntarily. Put your trust in something other than money during this exercise.

- *Subscribe to a Catholic Worker newspaper.*

Catholic Worker communities deal holistically with poverty, and especially homelessness. By just reading their newspaper you will learn a lot about the realities, causes, and just responses to poverty. Go to www.catholicworker.org to find the Catholic Worker community nearest you.

- *Buy a Christmas present for a child in foster care.*

In most states, little money is available for Christmas presents for foster children. Contact your state agency in charge of foster care and donate a present to a foster child.

- *Buy something through Co-op America.*

Go to www.coopamerica.org, click on shopping, and browse through all the different companies. Find something that you need and buy it through a company listed on their Web site.

- *Support labor unions*

Labor unions have historically been critical to improving the work conditions, wages, and hours of those on the bottom of the corporate ladder. Vote to support labor unions in your state, and support your own union if you are in one.

Twenty-minute activities

• *Learn about the demographics of the poor in your area.*

Helping to address the needs of the poor can begin with learning about their demographics in your area. Go to a search engine like www.google.com and type, for example, "poverty in Ohio." Find out what you can about the people living in poverty in your state.

• *Learn about welfare and public assistance.*

The public response to poverty is a complicated mess of various programs with different criteria, each one having a different application process—or at least this is the experience of many people. Spend twenty minutes researching what is available and how it works.

• *Attend a hearing or meeting with a poor person, and act as their witness or advocate.*

The poor are commonly treated harshly simply because they are poor. A friend of mine who works with the homeless has noticed that his mere presence when a homeless person attends a hearing makes for an improved outcome. Volunteer to be that witness for someone in your community. Call Catholic Charities, your parish, or the local Catholic Worker house to find the right place for you to help.

• *Learn the poverty level for a family the size of yours, and write out a budget.*

Go to www.hhs.gov, search for "poverty guidelines," and select the most recent listing. Find out the poverty level for your family. Write out a monthly budget using the money suggested by the guidelines. Imagine what it would be like to live on that budget.

• *Visit a Catholic Worker house.*

Putting the needs of the poor first is more powerful when we are face to face with the poor. Visit a Catholic Worker house and ask for a tour. You should call first so you don't arrive at an especially busy time. Look poor people in the eye, knowing you are looking at God's precious ones.

• *Reflect on the reason for this particular social justice teaching.*
Spend twenty minutes reflecting on why the poor and vulnerable are singled out as needing our attention and care. In your reflection, play the role of devil's advocate and argue with yourself.

• *Learn about criminal justice and the poor.*
I know a legislator who has been in law enforcement for thirty years. In a discussion about the death penalty and poverty, he pointed out that the poor are worse off than others at every level of the criminal justice system. Spend twenty minutes researching the role that poverty plays when a person finds himself or herself within the criminal justice system.

• *Reflect on the deserving versus undeserving poor.*
The teaching to care for the poor challenges our judgment that only the deserving poor are worthy of charity. It calls us to place *all* the poor first, not only the ones we deem worthy. Spend twenty minutes reflecting on what makes the poor deserving. Can you really put the needs of someone you consider undeserving first?

• *Learn about charity versus justice, and write out examples.*
Charity is what we do to help people who are victims of a broken system; justice is fixing the system. "When I gave food to the poor, they called me a saint. When I asked why the poor were hungry, they called me a Communist," said Archbishop Dom Helder Camara. Write down examples of charity and examples of justice. Try to balance your examples.

• *Visit a soup kitchen as a guest.*
Pretend you are poor or homeless and visit a soup kitchen as a guest. Don't worry that you are using their food; just go. If you feel guilty, just let the guilt be present. If you are uncomfortable, just let it be there. Enjoy the meal and go home.

- *In politics do you put the poor and vulnerable first or yourself first?*
The bite of this teaching is that the poor and vulnerable must come first for Christians. Most politicians run campaigns based on the needs of their constituents rather than the needs of the poor and vulnerable. Pay attention to your voting decisions and see if you contribute to politicians catering to middle class needs over the needs of the poor.

- *Find organizations that help the poor in your state and get on their legislative network.*
Call your state Catholic Conference and find out the organizations in your state that advocate for the poor. You can find a listing of state Catholic Conferences at www.nasccd.org. Get on their legislative network so you can contact key legislators at critical moments in support of legislation that puts the poor and vulnerable first.

- *Envision an economy or society that puts the poor first.*
Spend twenty minutes envisioning an economy or society that puts the poor first. What does it looks like? How does it work? How do things change over time? Write down your ideas.

- *Volunteer to do foster respite care or elder respite care*
People with more money can afford to hire babysitters or respite care workers, but the poor don't have that option. Volunteer to do respite care for foster children or the elderly. Contact your state's foster care agency or elderly agency to find opportunities.

Dignity of Work and Rights of Workers

The economy must serve people, not the other way around. Work is more than a way to make a living; it is a form of continuing partici-pation in God's creation. If the dignity of work is to be protected, then the basic rights of workers must be respected the right to productive work, to decent and fair wages, to organize and join unions, to pri-vate property, and to economic initiative.

U.S. Conference of Catholic Bishops

Most of us spend over half our waking life either at work or doing something for work, but we rarely think about how much God is with us in that work. Societal norms demand that we never be overtly religious at work. God lives at church, and God enters our homes at night when we say our prayers; but we are often blind to God at work. Even if we believe that God is in our workplace, we maintain our distance.

The truth is that God is there because God is everywhere: God is indeed in our workplace. God is in our work and working through our work. God is in our hands, our minds, our creativi-ty, our intelligence, and our eyes. God is a verb, not a noun. By cooperating with God in our work, we contribute to society in a way that is substantial and real. Pope John Paul II said: "The church is convinced that work is a fundamental dimension of man's existence on earth" (*Laborem exercens*, II. 4).

All work is creating; even the most mundane task creates something that wasn't there before. The grocery checker moves groceries and creates a transaction. The accountant creates financial records. The teacher creates a learning experience. God is the source of all creativity, and God co-creates with us.

While we usually think of work as employment, when the church talks about work, it has a much broader understanding of the word. Work is any activity "beginning in the human subject and directed toward an external object" (*Laborem exercens*, II. 4). Work is work regardless of its monetary status. A full-time parent works. A retired person works. A volunteer works. Workers work.

The church rejects the idea that work is basically an economic endeavor, where workers sell their labor in the marketplace. Instead, work is a fundamental part of the human condition. However, work is the way most people receive income to support themselves and their families. Intrinsic to our understanding of the holy nature of work is the idea that work and income must be balanced, that wages must be sufficient for workers to support their families at a decent level. It is against God's will when people work full-time and are not paid enough to get by.

Living out this teaching involves three arenas: our own work, our work environments, and the things we do that affect other people's work.

Five-minute activities

• *Be competent in your work.*

When you do your best at work, when you are open to growing and getting better, you are living out the best that God has to offer the world. So many people have benefited in this life from people who exercised the ministry of competence. Not only doctors and nurses need to be competent, but bus drivers, airplane pilots, machine operators, teachers, pastors, cooks, and so forth. Not being competent can have negative or even disastrous effects for those we serve. Conversely, when we are competent in our work, we contribute to the kingdom of heaven.

• **Work with vitality and moderation.**

Just as competence is part of the dignity of work and honesty is integral to that dignity, so, too, is working an honest day. When you are at work, really *work*; invest your energy, intelligence, and creativity. Be committed to why you are there. But working an honest day also demands that you remember you are more than your employment. Our society has progressively been moving toward a longer and longer work week, to the detriment of our corporate spirituality and family health. An honest day's work ends after eight hours.

• **Don't shop on Sunday.**

Many workers live at the whim of their employer's scheduling, especially those in lower-paid jobs. We have influence over that scheduling by reducing demand during certain times. By doing our shopping on Saturday or other days instead of on Sunday, we reduce demand on Sunday, so more workers will be able to use that day as one of rest.

• **Don't call any business at night.**

Following up on our influence on workers' schedules, many call centers operate 24/7 as well. The negative health effects of people working in the night are well documented. When I phone a call center at midnight, I am contributing in an indirect but real way to those health effects. It's true that police, firefighters, emergency workers, and health care workers need to work at night. But customer service reps who work for catalog or insurance companies do not.

• **Do work you love.**

It is an unfortunate reality that many people don't experience the holy grace in their own work. Instead, work feels like drudgery. It's something that you get through in order to get a paycheck.

The truth is that God doesn't want you to suffer, but God does want you to work. The lottery is not the solution; pursuing your passion is the solution. God gave you those holy passions. Find something you love to do, and then find somebody who will pay you to do it.

• **Respect the work of co-workers.**

Because work is holy and dignified, living an authentic life includes recognizing the dignity of other workers, especially the ones we work with. But sometimes respecting the people closest to us is the most difficult. Social justice is a whole lot easier when ideas are abstract. But the challenge of the gospel is to be real. Jesus didn't give us any wiggle room—he said it's not enough to think about it; we have to do it. It's hard, it's difficult, but it's the only way to follow Christ.

• **Treat workers as honest.**

People are very responsive to expectations. Parenting books speak a lot about this with children, but I doubt we ever grow out of it. If people treat us like we're honest, competent, and dedicated, then we tend to be that way. When workers are treated as honest people, they are that much more likely to see their own work as dignified.

• **Pay a living wage.**

For those who are in management positions, the need to pay a living wage is loaded with responsibility. Keep the vision, know the issues, and progress toward it. Even if you can't make it all the way, being Christian means you keep trying. Keep the pressure on yourself and your business to continue moving in the right direction toward paying a living wage.

• **Smile at people whose work is difficult; appreciate them.**

Unfortunately, many people in our society feel that work is a burden. They work only to pay the bills; if they could get out of working, they would. They don't see their work as contributing to society and they don't see the dignity or holiness inherent in their work. Simply smiling at these people, even if they don't smile back, makes a difference. There is a human connection: you are Jesus smiling at them, and they are Jesus in front of you.

- **Buy organic when possible.**

One easy and almost foolproof way of supporting economic justice is to buy organic. Not only are organic products produced in environmentally sounds ways, but organic producers tend to treat their workers in a more just way. This is part of the reason that organic products cost more; when you buy them, you are not only getting a bag of carrots, you are supporting people who are working the land and who earn a decent living. In addition, while pesticides may have a minor effect on consumers' health, they have a major effect on the farmworkers who are in the fields every day.

- **Buy locally-produced fruits and vegetables.**

In our age of expanding multinational corporations, small businesses are having more and more difficulty surviving. The family farm is especially under attack. At the grocery store, check labels to see where the produce is grown. Buy what is grown closest to you.

- **Buy from small, local businesses.**

Go out to eat at locally-owned restaurants (not chains). Get your car fixed at a garage where the business owner is the one doing the repairs. Fill your prescriptions at a locally-owned drug store. Buy your meat from a butcher who processes locally-grown meat.

- **Encourage others in their work.**

There are a million different ways that we can encourage others in their work: thank a receptionist for your messages, compliment a well-prepared marketing plan, thank a nurse for taking care of "your love," make a comment within earshot that the grocery store clerk was fast and efficient, drop your mechanic a note saying that your car is working great after the repair. Pay attention to the work that people do and appreciate both their good work and the effects of that work.

- **Treat all workers as professionals, not just the highly-paid or well-educated ones.**

We tend to put a lot of emphasis on credentials and income in our society: people with a college degree are professionals (white collar) and everyone else isn't (blue collar). The truth is that education and salary don't define us; our work is holy because of God. The work of those who harvest lettuce is just as crucial to our world as the work of the grocery chain CEO. When people at every level are treated as professionals, as uniquely qualified in their areas of expertise, they tend to take greater pride in their work.

• *Treat safety regulations as scripture; you could be saving your own and others' lives by following them.*
According to the U.S. Department of Labor, 5,524 workers died on the job in 2002, and 4.7 million more were injured. Many of those accidents were truly accidents; but sometimes accidents are the result of people willfully violating or ignoring safety regulations. Following safety requirements may seem like a waste of time, but it can be a matter of life or death.

Ten-minute activities

• *Write a letter to an elected official supporting a living wage.*
Write a letter to those who represent you (even if you didn't vote for them and don't intend to vote for them next time) saying that you want them to work for public policies that support living wages for all workers. Include your name, address, and phone number.

• *Write a letter to the CEO of a company where you shop to ask that he or she pay living wages to their employees.*
Think of one place where you spend money—the grocery store, bank, credit card company, department store—and write a letter to the CEO. Tell them that you are a customer and you want all their employees to be paid a living wage. Urge them to the do the right thing for the community. If you see a competitor doing a better job of paying a living wage, take your business there.

• *Join a union.*
Few people know that the labor movement in the United States wasn't going well until the Catholic church threw its weight behind

the unions. The unions have helped institute reforms such as the forty-hour workweek, minimum wage, time off on weekends, and safety rules. Unions continue to be one of the most effective means of protecting worker rights and achieving justice for workers.

• *Be active in your union.*

Vote in leadership ballots. Hold leaders accountable to their primary role of protecting and advocating for workers, including protecting the viability of workers' jobs.

• *Think of work as your vocation: are you where you belong?*

Work is holy because of God's participation in it; thus, work can truly be thought of as a vocation, a call by God to a specific purpose. When teachers think of teaching as a vocation, they approach their work differently. It becomes a ministry. *What* they do is the same, but *how* they do it is quite different. When you approach work as a vocation, God will whisper in your ear and let you know if you are in the right spot. God has given each of us our passions, and if we follow those passions with honesty and authentic conviction, the kingdom of God will be within our grasp.

• *Write a letter to the editor about the dignity of work.*

I once read that although politicians read most of their mail, they read *all* the letters to the editor in their local newspapers. Write a short letter to the editor (about 150 words) about your convictions regarding the dignity of work and the respect all workers deserve.

• *Support tax policies that are preferential for workers.*

When you see policies that seem slanted against workers, note your opposition. When you see tax policies that are good for workers, note your support for them. Just being aware of your own position will change the way you talk with your friends and colleagues, as well as inform the way you vote.

• *Write a letter to your legislators and congressmen telling them how much you care about the way public policies effect workers.*

Write a letter to your legislators expressing your opinion in this area. Many laws are regularly challenged. If your elected officials know that you want a law to stand, they will be more likely to fight to keep it. Never underestimate the influence you have over your elected officials.

• *Pray for the unemployed.*

We can sense the holiness of work, which is especially painful for those unable to work due to unemployment. Unemployment is difficult on people financially, but it can also be difficult emotionally and psychologically as well. Pray for those looking for work, that they remember the dignity of their work and how special they are to God.

• *Support work centers.*

Several groups of people are systematically excluded from the work force by prejudice: those coming out of prison; those coming off welfare; those who live on the streets; those being released from mental institutions; those trying to return to work after staying home with their children. Work centers help people obtain experience and education and build a work history. Look for a work center in your area. Help with their fund-raising efforts and buy from them.

• *Hire an ex-convict, a full-time parent returning to the workforce, a former welfare recipient, or another disadvantaged worker.*

After recognizing the discrimination some groups face as they try to get work, offer them a job (if you can). Ignore the "buts": but an ex-con might cheat me, a person coming off welfare might be lazy, a parent returning to the workforce might be ineffective. The truth is that many of these people will be wonderful, hard-working, dedicated, and very loyal workers because of the grace you showed them. Be part of creating a world where it's easy to be good. If you suffer for trying, then blessed are you for suffering on behalf of the kingdom.

Twenty-minute activities

- *Write out answers to these questions: Who is helped by my work? Who is hurt by my work?*

When we stay focused on the daily tasks, upcoming deadlines, and our immediate involvement, we often don't see the bigger picture. With some occupations we can easily see the people who benefit: teachers benefit their students, doctors benefit their patients, and farmers benefit those who eat their crops. But sometimes this is more difficult. If the only people helped by your work are those who benefit from your income, then you've got a problem—you're either not looking hard enough or your work is not contributing to the common good. Holy work helps somebody. But work can also hurt people when it makes money by exploiting other workers and feeding immoral urges like militarism, promiscuity, and materialism.

- *Form an occupational group in your parish.*

One of the criticisms of religion is that it often lacks relevance to people's lives. Social justice is about finding that relevance. Invite other workers to join a parish-based group to reflect on the faith elements of your work. Call the parish secretary, get a time and a location, and ask her to run an announcement in the bulletin for four weeks before your first meeting. Meet monthly to talk about what it means to be Christian in your line of work.

- *Spend some time noticing the dignity of your own work.*

As a spiritual exercise, spend twenty minutes at work noticing the holy dignity of your own work. Where is the dignity in your work? Where do you struggle to see dignity? Take a few notes and review them once in a while, adding more details as you continue to be open to this aspect of your work.

- *Spend some time being attentive to how God is operative in your work.*

As a spiritual exercise, spend twenty minutes at work noticing God in your work. Can you feel God with you as you type that letter?

Can you feel God at the meeting as ideas are bubbling up? Can you feel God in the strength and movement of your body?

• Find the face of one person who benefits from your work.

You can think abstractly about who is helped by your work, or you can have that abstract thought birthed into a real person. Find people who are helped by the work you do, not only by your income but by your actual work, and look at their faces. Look at them as Jesus would look at them; see them for the complete human beings they are. Say a prayer of thanks to God that you are able to help them.

• Think of somebody you saw working: Who is helped by their work? Who is hurt?

Just as you reflected on your own work, reflect on somebody else's. As you drive home, find one person working and think about who is helped by their work and who is hurt. Dorothy Day said that some jobs are immoral and cited anyone in the advertising or nuclear weapon industries. Do you think she was right? Why or why not?

• Learn about living wage.

Everybody has a different idea about what constitutes a living wage. A good Web site to help you become more informed is www.livingwagecampaign.org. Researching this topic will raise your consciousness. You'll find yourself making decisions based on what people need to survive (the common good) instead of what the marketplace allows (personal gain).

• Ask your pastor if parish workers are paid a living wage.

Call your pastor and tell him you've been reading about the church's teaching on living wage and you've done some research. Share what you have found so he can ensure that all who work for the parish are paid a living wage.

• Challenge the finance council on paying a living wage.

Call the members of your parish finance council and tell them you've been reading about the church's teaching on living wage. Share what you have found so they can ensure that all who work for the parish are paid a living wage.

Solidarity

We are our brothers' and sisters' keepers, wherever they live. We are one human family, whatever our national, racial, ethnic, economic, and ideological differences. Learning to practice the virtue of solidarity means learning that "loving our neighbor" has global dimensions in an interdependent world.

U.S. Conference of Catholic Bishops

Solidarity is a word with holy depth. Just using it in everyday language can rightly be called a spiritual exercise. Being in solidarity with someone makes their pains your pains, their struggles your struggles, and their victories your victories. Being in solidarity is to embrace a person with the embrace of the divine.

The sharp edge of this teaching is that we are called to solidarity with *all* people. Just because oppression is happening far away from us doesn't mean it isn't our problem.

This teaching calls us to see beyond borders. It calls us to see people everywhere as our neighbors and worthy of our love. This teaching gives weight to the need for paying a living wage to coffee growers. It makes environmental protection in the Amazon our issue. It makes the elimination of child labor throughout the world a vital concern for us.

This teaching calls us to see other people authentically, the way we see friends. We can easily condemn people who are different from ourselves, and yet be compassionate and merciful with our friends. But this teaching calls us to extend our compassion and mercy to those we don't know and may not agree with. It asks us never to reduce a human being to the present moment, but always to see the history and formation of a person and be watchful for the genuine person created by God straining to burst forth.

When we start to feel this solidarity we come to recognize our interdependence. Modern ears might perceive this dependence on people in the developing world in a paternalistic and superior way: I am dependent on them for my cup of coffee, and my cheap prices at Wal-Mart. We tell ourselves this, knowing full well we can live without any of these things.

If we are honest, we recognize our difficulty in admitting dependence, especially dependence on those whom we might consider less than ourselves. We like to think of ourselves as the ones who provide life-giving jobs, medicines, and technology, but we don't like to see that life-giving work comes the other way as well. The church teaches that it does; our challenge is to see our dependence and accept it.

Living this teaching involves both working for justice across the globe and building connections with people who are different than us.

Five-minute activities

• *Shop at a grocery store in a neighborhood that makes you uncomfortable.*

The gospel challenges us to be a neighbor to every person on earth. Stretch yourself by entering the place of people different from yourself, whether it be a poor neighborhood or a wealthy neighborhood.

• *Be kinder than necessary.*

It sounds like a cliché to say that we should be kinder than necessary, but it's not easy to do. We admire witty put-downs and the strength of competition. Yet solidarity means being one with someone else, seeing beyond the external behaviors to the human being inside. When we react with kindness, we build up what is good in the world and activate the glue that binds people together.

• Buy fair trade coffee.

Coffee is the second-largest traded commodity in the world, second only to oil. Some coffee has been certified fair trade, ensuring that the people producing it receive a living wage. If you can't find fair trade coffee in your local grocery store, you can buy it through Equal Exchange at www.equalexchange.org.

• Welcome the immigrant.

Thinking globally doesn't require that we go very far. Many communities already have significant immigrant populations. Be welcoming to them. Smile at immigrants. Be the arms of God welcoming them at the church doors. Go even further, if you can; become their friends.

• Talk about a group in the developing world and use "we" instead of "they."

Joining with others in solidarity means breaking down us/them thinking. Although using "them" when talking about groups of people different than yourself may be grammatically correct, it is a good spiritual exercise to use "we" instead. The goal is not to fool yourself into thinking you fully understand their lives, struggles, and glories, but rather to see things from their perspective.

• In war, count enemy deaths along with those of U.S. troops.

For many of us, living in solidarity involves extracting ourselves from the normal way of thinking. The news tends to report only U.S. military and civilian deaths. Living in solidarity means that every lost life is a tragedy and an occasion for sorrow. Pay attention to enemy deaths—both military and civilian—and figure those in your own count. Feel sorrow for those deaths, too.

• Express outrage at any U.S. support for violence.

In a democracy, the actions of our government are our responsibility. When the news uncovers any U.S. support for violence—like arms for the Sandinistas or the torture training at the School of the Americas in Georgia—express outrage. Speak out that we are a people whose moral values make no place for violence or the support of violence.

• **Respect the free choices of others.**

When we have little contact with people from far away places who live very different lives, we might assume they have the same wants, desires, and dreams as us. That's not always true. Practice the virtue of listening by being open to the dreams and aspirations of different people, and then support those dreams.

• **Join Catholic Relief Services' e-mail network.**

Go to www.catholicrelief.org and click on "E-mail Updates." By signing up, you'll automatically receive regular insider news and information from Catholic Relief Services. The regular updates will keep you aware of what is happening with the poor around the world and ways that you can help.

• **Exercise listening.**

Solidarity means standing peer-to-peer rather than the differential of the powerful to the weak. When we see someone as a friend or sister, genuine listening becomes a necessary and basic skill. But in our fast-paced world, we are much better at sending messages than receiving them. When you find yourself in the position of receiving a message, spend five minutes and just listen. Hear every word that is said. Make sure you understand the message.

• **Look for people you consider "other."**

As you go about your regular day, look for people you consider as "other." Look for people who are different from yourself—different race, different educational background, richer, poorer, who use a different language, and so forth. Just notice them; see them.

• **Banish condemning language from your politics.**

In today's polarized political landscape, the other side seems to be consistently painted as Satan incarnate. Let this stop with you. Instead of saying things like, "You have to be stupid to be Republican" or "You have to be amoral to be a Democrat," use language that supports the different choices of others without feeling that you have to agree with them. Let love be what binds you together, and let the differences of opinion be interesting rather than divisive.

- **At meal times, pray for the people who grew and packaged your food.**

When you pray at meal times, ask God to bless the food, those eating it, and those who grew it and delivered it to you. Chances are you will be praying for a great many people who have invested their energy into literally nourishing you.

Ten-minute activities

- **Write a letter condemning environmental degradation by U.S. companies in the third world.**

Write a letter to your congressmen condemning U.S. companies who degrade the environment in other parts of the world. Ask them to support or sponsor legislation that holds companies responsible for the same environmental protections elsewhere as they are held to in the United States. Do this for the love of God and the love of people living throughout the world.

- **Do your buying habits hurt those in other countries?**

Notice your buying habits: are you spending money in ways that encourage human degradation in developing countries? To argue that a job that pays ten cents an hour is better than no job is not valid. With so many choices to make when we shop, no one has to buy from companies with unjust labor practices. Spend ten minutes reflecting on your own buying patterns.

- **Does loving our neighbor mean giving them our culture?**

The number one American export is our culture via the entertainment industry. (Perhaps that is the source of so much anti-Americanism right now.) Spend ten minutes reflecting on how we can love our global neighbors without necessarily giving them our culture.

- **Write a letter supporting policies that prevent multinational companies from avoiding moral responsibility.**

Write a letter to your congressmen condemning multinational corporations that avoid moral responsibility for their actions abroad. Ask them to introduce legislation that holds companies accountable for their practices.

- **Support Catholic Relief Services (CRS).**

Go to www.crs.org and click on "Get Involved." There are many different ways that individuals, parishes, and schools can get involved in living in solidarity with people across the globe. Find one that fits within your life and do it.

- **Buy from CRS's fair trade catalog.**

Go to www.crsfairtrade.org and click on "Fair Trade Handicrafts." They have hundreds of beautiful and well-made items at reasonable prices. This is a great way to shop for gifts or household items. Get their catalog and place an order.

- **Write your congressmen condemning group selfishness.**

Placing priority on U.S. interests is actually nothing more than group selfishness. Write your congressmen condemning overemphasis on group selfishness, asking that they always work for win-win negotiations in foreign policy rather than only catering to U.S. national interests. This is an enormous step toward solidarity. Justice demands that we work for the common good rather than personal gain.

- **With your children, encourage love and care over being right.**

When being right is more important than loving people, solidarity breaks down. Talk with your children about placing more value on being loving than on being right. Be sure to comment when you see your children being loving, and especially compliment them when they give up being right in order to do so. Your positive encouragement will make an enormous difference.

- **Support public policies that take care of people.**

Spend ten minutes thinking about the public policies that care for people, both within and outside national borders: public education, welfare, Medicaid, Social Security, HIV/AIDS efforts, and so on. Reflect on your own support for these programs.

• *Buy something at Ten Thousand Villages.*

Ten Thousand Villages looks like a retail chain but it's actually a nonprofit outlet for third-world artisans. According to their Web site, Ten Thousand Villages provides vital, fair income to third-world people by marketing their handicrafts and telling their stories in North America. Visit their web site at www.tenthousandvillages.com to find a store near you.

Twenty-minute activities

• *Take your kids to play in a park on the other side of town.*

The next time you take your kids to the park, go to a park on the other side of town. The children will enjoy the different playground and you will discover that places away from home can also be safe. You will have seen another face of God in these people.

• *Attend local festivals.*

Many cities have local festivals that highlight diversity within the community. Find out when one is being held, put it on the calendar, attend, and have fun. Enjoy the sights, music, and smells while experiencing the richness of diversity.

• *Attend interfaith events.*

Expressing our love of God with people from other faith traditions builds solidarity with them and strengthens our commitment to our own faith. It gives us sensitivity to the beliefs of other people—beliefs that are held just as strongly as our own. By attending interfaith events, we enter an environment that supports and uplifts everyone's faith tradition. We are free to appreciate other people's traditions while fully embracing our own.

• *Plan a trip.*

It is easier to live in solidarity with people whom we have actually met. Plan a trip for your next vacation and use it as an opportunity to put yourself in another environment. Simply enjoying yourself away from home helps to see beyond your own horizon.

• Learn about the School of the Americas.

For many, the work against torture and nuclear proliferation begins on U.S. soil. The School of the Americas (SOA) protest held every November at Fort Benning, Georgia, attracts thousands of people to protest a U.S.-funded school whose graduates have committed some of the worst atrocities in Latin America. Learn about the protest at www.soaw.org.

• Support protesters at the SOA.

In 2004 fifteen protesters at Fort Benning crossed the line and were arrested. Go to www.soaw.org, click on "Take Action," and then "Prisoners of Conscience." Find out what you can do to support people incarcerated for civil disobedience.

• Visit an event at a mosque.

Fifty years ago, the "other" in our collective lives was the Communists. In 2006, it is the Muslims. In an effort to help people understand the teachings of Islam, many Islamic communities are inviting the public to mosque events. For example, in my hometown the Muslim community invited the public to the weekly dinners during Ramadan when they broke their fast. Call the local mosque, ask about events open to the public, and attend.

• Participate in Operation Rice Bowl this Lent.

Catholic Relief Services has an easy and free program that helps parishes and families learn about hunger in the world. This lenten program includes prayer, fasting, almsgiving, and learning. To order your free copy of the program, visit www.crs.org and click on "Get Involved" and "Operation Rice Bowl."

• Assume that every terrorist event occurs because people feel helpless. Search for the reason why.

When other people's actions don't make sense, use the kindness of your heart to assume there is more to the story rather than dismissing them as crazy. As a spiritual exercise, spend twenty minutes with the assumption that terrorism is the last ditch action of a person who feels totally helpless. Explore, in your own mind, why they might feel helpless. This exercise doesn't require that you believe the story, only that you assume it for twenty minutes.

• *Forgive those who have wronged you.*
Sometimes solidarity can be the most difficult with people who have hurt you. Spend twenty minutes reflecting on someone who is difficult to forgive. Think about what would it would take to make reconciliation possible. If reconciliation is unlikely, keep your reflection on your own willingness to offer forgiveness.

• *Invite other people to dinner.*
Connecting with people outside our daily lives can be done in lots of little ways. Invite someone over for dinner. It's not a big deal. It's easy. Just make a casual dinner, enjoy some comfortable conversation, and don't try to accomplish anything else.

• *Exercise the virtue of love over being right.*
Think about your own need to be right over being loving. In one situation, allow yourself to be loving instead of being right, and then reward yourself for your spiritual fortitude. Although many opportunities will present themselves, being able to catch those situations requires spiritual discipline. In that moment, you will be standing with Christ who always put loving first.

• *Use your retirement savings and investments to build up others.*
Talk with your financial advisor and insist that they provide you with socially responsible investment opportunities. Visit www.socialinvest.org. Find a fund (or funds) that fit into your financial plan, and know that you are using your resources to live the virtue of solidarity. You'll find that social responsibility isn't necessarily detrimental to your investment goals.

THEME 7

Care for God's Creation

We show our respect for the Creator by our stewardship of creation. Care for the earth is not just an Earth Day slogan, it is a requirement of our faith. We are called to protect people and the planet, living our faith in relationship with all of God's creation. This environmental challenge has fundamental moral and ethical dimensions that cannot be ignored.

U.S. Conference of Catholic Bishops

A friend of mine is an avid recycler who not only recycles her own stuff, but will happily take anybody else's. When rescuing paper from the trash, she quips that St. Peter counts every sheet. We all chuckle, but what if she's right?

All around us is the evidence of God's love and creative power. Whether looking at the microscopic level or the cosmic level, the wonder of God's creation is more than the human mind can fully comprehend. But the power of nature can be overshadowed by the relentless onslaught of people when we physically abuse it and destroy it with our pollution.

With our Americanized notion of land ownership, we might easily forget that human beings do not own land: the land belongs to God. We hold the land in trust for a short while, but faithfulness reveals that God is our landlord: "For the land is mine; with me you are but aliens and tenants" (Leviticus 25:23). Respect and love for the Creator is revealed in our tender and loving care of creation.

Many of us live in urban environments with little resemblance to the natural places they once were. When every tree we see is surrounded by concrete, our experience of creation can feel diminished. But whether surrounded by concrete or not, every tree is a work of creation. Every human being is a work of creation. The water we drink and the air we breath are works of creation. The food that sustains us is a work of creation.

Creation is all around us if only we have eyes to see. How much easier it is to see when we are plunged into a Rocky Mountain forest, a natural coastline, or the Everglades. As our blindness wears off, we start to see nature in nooks and crannies where we never looked before. Its diversity and complexity provoke awe and wonder.

When we hear, "fill the earth and subdue it; and have dominion over the fish of the sea and over the birds of the air and over every living thing that moves upon the earth" (Genesis 1:28), it must be heard as a message not only for this generation, but for generations throughout all time. Our care for the earth is not some New Age idea; it is grounded in our faith. God created this earth for all of humankind and our dedication to our maker means that we preserve and protect the world for the future. Using up resources and destroying nature for our benefit today while ignoring the needs of future generations is sacrilegious.

Caring for God's creation includes both protecting nature and expanding our awareness of the preciousness of creation.

Five-minute activities

• *Combine wash loads.*
Water is precious and necessary for just about every part of living. When we experience the waters of baptism, we are reminded of its life-saving and irreplaceable quality. Conserve water by

combining wash loads. The extra effort to save water helps us care for God's creation.

• *Conserve electricity.*

When I was a child, my parents told us constantly to turn off the lights to save money. Today, many people no longer need to save electricity for financial reasons, but the principle is still a good one. Turn off the lights when you leave the room. Don't leave appliances on when you're not using them. Think of other ways you can reduce electricity usage.

• *Buy organic.*

Raising food without chemicals is good for the environment, good for the farmworkers who are exposed to chemicals, and good for the earth with the added benefit of conservation. Organic food keeps us grounded in the preciousness of food. The food has been raised with care, and although it costs more, it often tastes better. This week buy one organic food that you didn't buy last week. It might be a gallon of milk or a head of lettuce. This one little change will have a positive effect.

• *Consume less.*

Our society's idea of success is that we consume whenever and wherever we want: more is better. Consuming less feels like moving down in social class. But respecting and loving the Creator means that we may only consume what we need. Every desire does not need to be fulfilled. This week, find one thing you can do without, and make a conscious decision not to buy it.

• *Notice the weather.*

Just like the diversity in life, the weather is constantly changing. Being aware of the weather means being more attuned to nature. Notice the weather today. If a storm blows over and the sun shines brightly, take a few moments to simply enjoy it.

• *Next time you buy a car, opt for a model that gets higher mileage.*

We use a lot of energy, especially for our cars, but every mile is not "created equal." Some cars use more gas than others. The next time you buy a car, make mileage an important factor—not because of the expense of gasoline, but because of the cost to the environment. Research different models to determine which one gets the best mileage, and buy that one.

• Use low-wattage bulbs.

Low-wattage light bulbs make conserving electricity easy while still giving off plenty of light. Buy a few so that the next time you need to replace a bulb, you've already got one on hand.

• Reuse things: clothes, notepaper, toys, and so forth.

Throwing things away is so easy that simply reusing things takes conscious thought. Instead of buying notepads, reuse scrap paper. Instead of throwing toys away when your children grow out of them, donate them to the Society of St. Vincent de Paul. Instead of throwing clothes away, donate them to a homeless shelter. Keep the packing materials from your next online order and reuse them.

• Buy recycled stuff.

Our purchasing dollar is powerful. When you have the option of buying recycled paper or folders, buy recycled. When you have the option to buy recycled plastic, buy recycled. Being part of creating a market for recycled goods means truly caring for God's creation.

• Avoid disposables.

Our dependence on disposable items seems to be increasing. The proliferation of disposable housecleaning products means you can wash the dishes, mop the floor, dust the house, clean the toilet, and just throw the cleaners away. The way we eat involves so much more waste than it used to—even drinking water now involves throwing away a plastic bottle. Today, find one disposable item you can avoid, and do so.

• Breast-feed your baby.

If you have a choice, be like Mary and breast-feed your baby. Give the words of Isaiah power over you, words spoken to Israel about the abundance of God: "You may nurse and be satisfied from her consoling breast; that you may drink deeply with delight from her glorious bosom" (Isaiah 66:11).

- ***Don't smoke, drink, or abuse your body.***

Loving God and caring for God's creation includes caring for your body. Choose to treat yourself with the loving care of the Creator and don't do anything to degrade yourself. You are a temple of the Holy Spirit. If you abuse your body by smoking or drinking or in any other way, make the decision right now to find a way to stop.

- ***Fix broken things instead of buying new ones.***

When Wal-Mart is having a sale on VCRs, we might be tempted to buy a new VCR instead of fixing the old one. But when that new VCR comes home, the old one goes in the trash. When we fix things, we conserve the earth's resources. Fixing things also has the benefit of supporting local businesses because most fix-it shops are locally owned.

- ***Buy local.***

Things that come from far away (i.e., imports) require lots of energy to transport. Even if they are cheaper, there is a cost in transportation that diminishes the earth. Buy things produced locally, knowing that you are saving energy.

Ten-minute activities

- ***Use public transportation or carpool.***

If your life includes a regular and predictable drive to work each day, finding alternative transportation just one day a month makes a difference. But don't stop at your commute. Any time you go somewhere, using public transportation or carpooling adds up to energy conservation and environmental protection.

- ***Examine your own water usage.***

Water is precious, necessary for life and for our economy. Reducing your water usage by just a little bit is a significant way to conserve this precious resource. Begin by simply paying attention to how much water you use. If you have a meter that measures water, record how much water you use each day.

- *Examine your energy usage.*

A prolonged power outage makes us realize how much we rely on electronic energy in our daily lives. Without electricity, we can't watch television, use the computer, or have light in the evening. Without electricity, many can't even heat their homes or cook. Our dependency on the energy provided by creation deserves respect. Pay attention to the way you use energy.

- *Make gas cost twice as much as it does.*

Our cars are useless without gas. Because many of us do not suffer financial pressure, we must rely on something else to motivate us to support conservation. Up the ante and let financial pressure work on you. For one week pretend that gas costs twice as much as it does by actually paying double. Whenever you fill your tank, write a check for the same amount to an environmental charity. Let the financial pressure change your behavior.

- *Eat natural food.*

Everything we eat is a harvest of creation, but many foods have gone through unnatural changes from their original state before entering our mouths. We were designed to be sustained with food designed by the Creator. Spend ten minutes making a plan that everything you eat for one day will be natural. Eating things that don't come in packages is an easy way, but just reading labels closely will help you avoid things like hydrogenated vegetable oil, high fructose corn syrup, or red dye #3.

- *Listen to music (or make music).*

As visual creatures, we can forget the things God creates that can't be touched. Making music and appreciating music requires the intervention of the divine—after all, it's just sound waves. But with the touch of God, those sounds waves become beautiful, meaningful, and evocative. Spend ten minutes in awe at the majesty of God communicated through music co-created with human beings.

• Avoid using chemicals in your yard.

We human beings alter nature in our landscaping. We select what plants will be allowed and the others we call weeds. We've taken this idea of controlling nature another step with the use of chemicals. But we now know that those chemicals can have an impact on nature far away from our homes. This summer, use organic fertilizer instead of chemical fertilizer. Pull a weed instead of using weed killer. Beautiful landscaping doesn't require environmental degradation. Gardens Alive (www.gardensalive.com) sells organic yard and garden products.

• Reset your thermostat.

Reset your thermostat one degree closer to the outside temperature—cooler in the winter and warmer in the summer. That little adjustment will have a significant change on your energy usage over time. Use clothing rather than energy to be comfortable. Enjoy your connection with the weather by being that much closer to it.

• Get a low-flow shower head.

Conserving water can be as easy as using different fixtures. The next time you are at the home center, spend ten minutes finding a low-flow showerhead, and install it in your shower. Showerheads are easy to install; using a low-flow one will save significant amounts of water over time.

• Protect your things so they last longer.

Conservation includes things we don't always associate with conservation. Protect your things so they last longer: cover your patio furniture over the winter, keep your car rust-free, bring in toys from the yard each night, and so forth.

• Make conservation a game for your children.

Tell your children that when they turn the lights off, they are helping to care for God's creation. Teach them to recycle their paper. Make sure they turn the water off when they are done washing up. Make it a game for them to find new ways to care for God's creation.

- **Stargaze.**

Part of living out this social teaching is to see the wonder and beauty of this creation we care for. Go outside for ten minutes tonight and look up at the stars. If you live in a big city, the next time you find yourself in the country at night, take ten minutes to stargaze. Look up at the majesty of creation that extends far beyond the boundaries of our own planet, our own solar system, even our own galaxy.

Twenty-minute activities

- **Recycle.**

If you don't already recycle at home, now is the time to get started. Take twenty minutes setting up a recycling center or well-placed bags or baskets around the house. Figure out how you're going to get your recycled stuff to a recycling center.

- **Take your chemicals and batteries to a Household Hazardous Waste disposal site.**

Most households generate some amount of hazardous waste that is potentially damaging when it gets to the landfill. Separate the batteries, paint, motor oil, and chemicals from your regular trash. Dispose of them when there is a local household hazardous waste day, or call the landfill to find out if they have a household hazardous waste collection point. Your twenty-minute effort will protect the earth and future generations.

- **Exercise.**

Exercise is a proven technique for caring for your body. This can be jogging or biking, working out at a gym, going for a walk in your neighborhood, swimming, or hiking. Find something you enjoy doing and do it often.

- **Use indigenous plants in your landscape.**

Plants that are native to your area need less care (that is, less water and chemicals) because the conditions are already perfect for them. Spend twenty minutes on the Internet researching indigenous plants or call your county cooperative extension plan to incorporate one new plant into your landscaping this year.

- **Take a walk outside.**

Getting yourself outside on a regular basis builds connections with the natural world. Walking forces us to move more slowly than we are accustomed to moving. Today, spend twenty minutes walking outside. Smell the air. Look at the sky. Feel the breeze on your face. Hear the sounds of birds.

- **Take a trip to to the forest or the ocean.**

For me, God is powerfully present in the grandeur of unadulterated nature in the forest or the ocean or the mighty rivers. Plan a trip to gaze on the face of God revealed through natural beauty.

- **Investigate solar or wind energy for your home.**

Our use of electricity doesn't have to degrade the environment. Spend twenty minutes investigating "green" energy sources for your own home. Even if you only generate twenty percent of your energy with solar panels or wind turbines, that is a lot of energy not coming from coal plants or river dams. Some power companies offer green energy so you can use this type of energy without the capital expense.

- **Reflect on your own materialism and consumption.**

Living out the teaching to care for God's creation involves self-reflection on our own habits of materialism and consumption. Our culture pushes us into the idea that consuming more is better, thus supporting the idea that we are what we own. Spend twenty minutes reflecting on how much these ideas influence you. Write down your own ideas and beliefs about materialism, and see how they affect your life.

- **Plant a garden.**

We may think that creation happened a long time ago and now it's done. But the truth is that God goes on creating all the time. Be present to the wonder of God by growing a garden that provides food for your family. If you don't have a spot for a garden, a simple pot is enough to grow leaf lettuce for sandwiches or salads.

• Go camping.

When you go camping, not only do you get yourself out into a natural environment, but everything about daily living changes. You have to carry water. You have cook over a fire. You have to dress for being outside. Camping takes us into the heart of nature and for that time conservation becomes natural.

• Carry all water for a day.

As a spiritual exercise to appreciate the preciousness of water, carry all your water for a day (except maybe the toilet). When you wash your hands, go to the kitchen to fill a bucket and carry it to the bathroom to use. When you cook, fill a bucket in the bathroom and carry it to the kitchen. When you bathe, fill a bucket in the kitchen or outside and carry it to the tub. By connecting every bit of water you use with the effort to carry it, your own water usage becomes that much more obvious.

• Examine your needs versus wants; be guilt-free for using the things you need.

In trying to live simply and walk lightly on the earth, some people develop unhealthy guilt over everything they use. Spend twenty minutes writing down things you use in life that are needs and things that are wants. Give yourself permission to be guilt-free about using those things you need. God really did create this wonderful earth to sustain and care for us.

• Bicycle or walk instead of driving your car.

Find one occasion this month when you can bicycle or walk instead of driving your car. You will conserve gas, exercise, and be outdoors. Doing it just once a month can be meaningful and valuable.

• Compost.

Anyone with a yard can do composting. Collect all plant waste—things like grass clipping, leaves, and vegetable trimmings—and dump them in a pile. Selecting a sunny location will help. Now and then, mix up your pile. In about a year, all that waste will be wonderful compost for the yard. Using a compost maker from the home center will speed the process up.

- **Visit the zoo.**

A visit to the zoo is a way to expose yourself to the vastness of God's creation without traveling. Plan a trip to the zoo for your family with the expectation of seeing God face to face in the animals there.

- **Pretend that poverty rules you.**

Consumption is part of wealth. The poor don't have any option but to get by with less. Let that reality rule you for the day. Let the Depression-era slogan be yours: "Use it up, wear it out, fix it up, make do."